AYRTON SENNA

Other books by the same author:

AYRTON SENNA
The Second Coming

AYRTON SENNA
The hard edge of genius

GERHARD BERGER
The Human Face of Formula 1

MICHAEL SCHUMACHER
Full drama of the 1994 World Championship

JAMES HUNT
Portrait of a Champion

TORVILL AND DEAN
The full story

TWO WHEEL SHOWDOWN!
The full drama of the races which decided the
World 500cc Motor Cycle Championship from 1949

GRAND PRIX SHOWDOWN!
The full drama of the races which decided
the World Championship 1950–92

Patrick Stephens Limited, an imprint of Haynes Publishing, has published authoritative, quality books for more than a quarter of a century. During that time the company has established a reputation as one of the world's leading publishers of books on aviation, maritime, motor cycle, car, motorsport, and railway subjects. Readers or authors with suggestions for books they would like to see published are invited to write to: The Editorial Director, Patrick Stephens Limited, Sparkford, Nr Yeovil, Somerset BA22 7JJ.

AYRTON SENNA
The Legend Grows

CHRISTOPHER HILTON

Patrick Stephens Limited

First published in 1995

British Library Cataloguing-in-Publication Data:
A catalogue record for this book is
available from the British Library.

ISBN: 1 85260 527 8

Library of Congress catalog card no. 95-76125

Patrick Stephens Limited is an imprint of Haynes Publishing, Sparkford, Nr Yeovil, Somerset BA22 7JJ.

Designed and typeset by G&M, Raunds, Northamptonshire.
Printed in Britain by Butler & Tanner Ltd, London and Frome.

Contents

1 To every thing there is a season, and a
time to every purpose under the heaven

2 A time to be born, and a time to die; a time to
plant, and a time to pluck up that which is planted

3 A time to kill, and a time to heal; a time to break
down, and a time to build up

4 A time to weep, and a time to laugh; a time to
mourn, and a time to dance

5 A time to cast away stones, and a time to gather
stones together; a time to embrace, and a time to
refrain from embracing

6 A time to get, and a time to lose; a time
to keep, and a time to cast away

7 A time to rend, and a time to sew; a time to keep
silence, and a time to speak

8 A time to love, and a time to hate; a time of war,
and a time of peace

Ecclesiastes, Chapter 3

Author's Introduction

*I*t's been a long year since yesterday afternoon, an afternoon which began hot and dry and sunny and ended deep in mourning. It's been a long year since 1 May 1994 which began with foreboding and compressed itself into 1.8 seconds, a moment which has expanded into all time.

A voracious industry built itself upon the death of Ayrton Senna at the San Marino Grand Prix, Imola, and mostly this industry travelled backwards into the well-recorded milestones of his life. There are exceptions, but not many. I have found only four: two books and two newspaper articles.

Let's be clear. You can, if you wish, pore over the times of every lap that Ayrton Senna drove at every Grand Prix meeting. This enormity of statistics exists, each recorded to three decimal places. You can revisit a goodly portion of those Grands Prix on video. You can sink waist-deep into thousands of newspaper and magazine cuttings, although a high percentage of them say the same thing. You can assemble your own library of books about him: there are currently some 40 worldwide. It is entirely possible, this spring of 1995, to fill a medium-sized art gallery with drawings, sketches, portraits, posters and paintings of him; and each week brings more, as artists everywhere try to redefine the image.

Photographic archives heave with filing cabinets full of their own images – all but his most intimate, secluded and precluded moments are somewhere in there. John Townsend, a noted Formula 1 photographer, estimates that about 250 photographers attend each Grand Prix and, taking his own work-rate as typical, each will use around 40 rolls of film. That's 36 pictures per roll or 360,000 images *per Grand Prix*. Only a fraction are of Senna, of course, but he drove 161 races.

In his 34 years, Senna grew into an immensity representing many things to many people: but he was only human, never claimed to be more or less.

Time gives perspective to what seems like only yesterday afternoon. I declare a personal interest. I wrote the first book to appear on him, *The Hard Edge of Genius* (which he said you could rely on) and wrote another, subtitled *The Second Coming* (which appeared the week before 1 May 1994). Both books were, I knew, incomplete, as all books written by one human being about another have to be. He was a bewildering subject, anyway. He'd have been a *very* unnerving interview for a psychiatrist, who might have required counselling afterwards. This book is also incomplete and no apologies for that. It seeks to explain the haunting, strange, almost inexplicable events before, during and after San Marino; it seeks to explain some of what lay behind the milestones across his 34 years, using material which is new or rarely seen.

The chapter headings were not laboriously chosen to reflect the mystical. They just fitted. Make of that what you will, just as you must with the subtitle *The Second Coming*, that week before Imola. There is a surprising amount of religion in this book. I didn't push the text that way, it moved there quite naturally.

In sum, I went looking and what follows is what I found.

Sincere thanks to David Chappell, Sports Editor of *The Times*, for permission to quote from their feature by Andrew Longmore on Senna's last weekend. I have unashamedly used it as part of the structure of Chapter Two. Most newspaper articles are destined to last 24 hours, until the next edition of the newspaper. This one was a dimension above that and deserves a better fate. Thanks equally to Derek Warwick, Johnny Herbert, Philippe Streiff, Peter de Bruyn, Mike Wilson; Mark Burgess of *Karting* magazine for active assistance and permission to quote; Joe Saward of *Formula 1 News* (formerly of *Autosport*); John Corsmit of the FIA; Pino Allievi of *La Gazzetta dello Sport*; Reinhold Joest; Gerhard Berger; E. L. Gordon for keeping a watchful eye on what appeared in the United States; Professor Sid Watkins; Frank Williams and Ann Bradshaw of Williams GP Engineering; The Bishop of Truro, Michael Ball; Lake Speed; Martin Whitaker, Press Delegate of the FIA, for candour and setting several important records straight; Owen O'Mahony, Senna's pilot; photographer John Townsend; Betise Assumpcao who handled Senna's publicity and gave me her time to check the accuracy of many facts; Angelo Parilla; Monica Meroni of Minardi, for active assistance and translation; Roland Christen; Dr. Giovanni Gordini of the Maggiore Hospital; the Liverani family; the staff at Imola; Gordon Message, John Love, Bob Dance, Rubens Barrichello, Marcel Gysin, Cor Euser; David Fern of Donington; David Tremayne, formerly of *Motoring News*; Rick Rinaman, a chief mechanic with the Penske team; Wilma Shalliday, Headmaster's Secretary, Loretto; Brian Hart; Simon Taylor for allowing me to quote from *Autosport;* and Inga for translations.

For permission to quote from their letters to me, I'm indebted to Lyn Patey for her care and candour, Jennifer Riley, Carolynne Kristina, Marcel van der Nol, Pam Jones, Renee Sharp, Mrs G. Robey, Wendy Thomas, Grietje Swater, Jenny Coles, Susan Nichols and Laura Giglio.

In compiling this book I have drawn background from several published works, *Ayrton Senna, Trajectoire D'un Enfant Gate* by Lionel Froissart (Glenat, Grenoble); *Adriane: My Life with Ayrton* by Adriane Galisteu (Apa Publishing, Adelaide); *Goodbye Champion, Farewell Friend* by Karin Sturm (English language edition, MRP, London); *Le Livre d'Or de la Formula 1 1994* by Renaud de Laborderie (Solar, Paris); *Damon Hill Grand Prix Year* by Hill and Maurice Hamilton (Macmillan, London); and *Flying On The Ground* by Emerson Fittipaldi and Elizabeth Hayward (William Kimber, London). Each brought aspects to the whole.

The illustrations are by Sporting Pictures (UK) Ltd. unless otherwise stated, and particular thanks to Crispin Thurston in helping with their selection. Thanks also to the other photographic agencies who have contributed, for their care in searching out unseen or little known material. John Stoneham (formerly of the *Adelaide News*) kindly provided the Second Coming cartoon.

CHAPTER ONE

A time
to speak

*E*verything which followed the beginning of the end – 2.18 on 1 May 1994 – moved in sequence, each slower than the one before, and they did not end with the completion of the official report into what befell Ayrton Senna during the San Marino Grand Prix. That report, available in February 1995, was of some 500 pages and prolonged a mystery as well as launching the next sequence: it was passed to magistrates in Bologna – the nearest large town to Imola, where the race had been run – and they then initiated a process of questioning participants and witnesses. Later, a trial judge would consider whether prosecutions be brought.

Nobody, surely, had anticipated a clean, swift conclusion and there were precedents. Two racing accidents involving fatalities in Italy – Wolfgang von Trips and 13 spectators in 1961, Jochen Rindt in 1970 – begat investigations which lingered and lumbered for years. But the death of Senna was different. He was arguably the most famous, and certainly the most fascinating, sportsman on the planet. His face was universally familiar. There must have been a couple of billion viewers who had watched the San Marino Grand Prix on television and witnessed Senna's Williams car go into a concrete wall at a corner called Tamburello, or seen replays of it on countless news bulletins, hour after hour, day after day. A very great imperative existed to know what had happened and why.

After the accident, the car had been impounded at the circuit where it remained while a magistrate, Maurizio Passarini, launched the official investigation. He brought a wide-ranging group of experts in to help and advise, because much of the investigation would penetrate the extremely technical. Whatever Passarini's deliberations and discoveries, however, several theories already existed about the cause, notably that the steering column on the Williams had failed, rendering Senna helpless.

A Grand Prix racing car is a highly complex creation. Sheer technology allows the most astonishing and exact information about its every movement (called telemetry) to be relayed to the pits. Patrick Head, the Williams Technical Director, had limited access to the crashed car but he and the Williams team tried to help, albeit from their factory in England. "We gave a comprehensive report on the telemetry from the steering wheel and did a lot of tests which we recorded on video. We presented documentation within a month of the accident which pretty much showed that we couldn't get any of the data that was recorded without the wheel being attached to the column.

"We then produced a report about two months later because, although we had given quite a lot about what we didn't think had happened, we thought it was important to give an opinion on what we did think happened. I asked our (Italian) lawyer what the response was on those reports and he said 'the problem is that both reports are too technical to be understood.' Well, the first had a few numbers in, but the second was deliberately put into layman's terms." Head, incidentally, saw the impounded wreckage only twice in the months after Imola, and then only for between five and 10 minutes.

In August, two French newspapers – *L'Equipe* and *Info-matin* – claimed to have a leak from the University of Bologna, which was active in the investigation, implying (it's an imprecise leak, don't forget) that a fracture in the steering column had been found or a quality flaw or a lack of thickness in the metal used. The Williams team responded within hours. "Current media reports giving information regarding the possible cause of Ayrton Senna's accident are not based on the official findings of the technical experts investigating the matter. They have not yet reached any conclusions and have asked the magistrates for a delay until the end of September. Therefore any speculation prior to this date is unfounded. We have no further comment."

The end of September 1994 came and went, and Passarini talked of his experts meeting "after the end of November." That came and went too, and so did Christmas, and so did January 1995. In early February, Max Mosley, President of the sport's ruling body, the FIA, said: "I expect the report will give an explanation for the causes of the accident and say that the steering column was broken. It will also probably mention the bumps on the track, which we all know about, but not much more. I expect it will blame some people, but I am satisfied in my own mind that no-one did anything that could be seen as deliberate or reckless with Senna's car. Everything was done with the best of intentions and no-one should be blamed for anything on moral grounds." Mosley added that he saw "no possibility of (Frank) Williams going to jail or the Williams team being put out of business." Quite how Mosley could say this is unclear.

In mid-February, Patrick Head said: "We have a copy of what is supposedly the experts' report going to the magistrate. I hesitate to make too much comment, but I cannot actually believe that the technical people who I am aware were involved had any influence on it. It does not appear to have anything like the structure of somebody with a technically-trained mind." A few days later, word leaked from Italy that the report contained a conclusion: the steering column had been shortened before the race – so that Senna had a better driving position and perhaps a better view of the cockpit instruments – and a length of tubing welded to the column. This snapped at the entry to Tamburello. Williams's Italian lawyer responded "our data shows the steering was working until the moment of impact."

And there it lay, as the final sequence of interviewing the participants and witnesses began. There it lay while so many people waited to know conclusively the what and the why of Tamburello, and could never find peace within themselves until they did.

CHAPTER TWO

A time of war and a time of peace

*T*he week leading to the 1994 San Marino Grand Prix at Imola began, as it seemed, in the most ordinary way. On Tuesday, 26 April, Ayrton Senna took his own plane, a British Aerospace HS125 and was flown by his own pilot, Owen O'Mahony, from Faro in southern Portugal – where he had a house – to Munich. Senna had a meeting there about his Audi distributorship in Brazil.

On the Thursday, O'Mahony flew Senna from Munich to Padua, a large city 32 kilometres from Venice. During the journey, O'Mahony says, Senna was "fine, perfectly OK." A long day, this. Senna was due at the launch of a mountain bike – built by an Italian company, Carraro – bearing his name. He went to the factory where, naturally, the employees made a fuss of him. He shook a lot of hands and was taken to the Sheraton Hotel, a typically modern building set in its own gardens amid gentle countryside five kilometres from Padua. There, in the Congress Centre – a large room on the ground floor – he played an active part in the launch. The Sheraton was precisely the place for this: crisp, functional, accepting business meetings effortlessly, a haunt of endless men in dark suits speaking the language of salesmanship, making (if you'll allow me a phrase) the big wheel turn.

Although the mountain bike was built by Carraro it bore a distinctive red *S* and, in white, the name Senna on its frame. For some time Senna had looked beyond his career and was engaged in creating a proper business empire. It embraced a cartoon magazine about himself, *Senninha*, based on his own exploits, and the proceeds from which were intended to help deprived children; the Audi cars; a joint venture with an Italian company for manufacturing domestic appliances; the manufacture of luxury yachts; a company which licensed Senna's own name and the stylised letter *S* to denote that. The bike was a further part of this empire, another step into the future. Senna was 34 and nearer the end of his career as a driver than the beginning. He could race against time but even he couldn't beat it; and with such a man there would have to be a proper, fulfilling next life. Hence, already, the empire. He left nothing to chance.

When they retire, most sportspeople hold to what they know. They become coaches or managers, they write for newspapers, they commentate on radio and television. The motor racing driver can prolong his career into sportscars or touring cars until his late 40s and use his name to establish car dealerships, which is logical and only one step removed from his career. I do not know a single person in *any* sport who has attempted a business empire of such breadth and scope as Senna.

Senna looked, as he always did on such occasions, perfectly groomed. He wore a crisply-cut well-fitting jacket, a creamy shirt and a sober tie nicely knotted so that the knot nestled within the flaps of the collar. Nothing garish, nothing to disturb the tone. Senna understood such details and, astonishingly, could play the chameleon, blending to circumstances while never sacrificing who or what he was. Equally astonishing, and just this once, he'd been chewing some gum and as he took his place on the stage Betise Assumpcao, his Press Relations lady, gestured. He realised and whipped it smartly out. Overall, he looked not quite a born business-man, but well on the way. He wasn't ready for the complete transition yet. He was balancing the past which had made him so immense, the present so rich with pos-sibilities, and the future which he was now bringing under his grip.

Some tentative reports suggest he was "nervous" as the launch began. That was when, at least in public, the ordinariness comes into question. We will have to deal with it as best we can. As a young man he'd been shy, introspective, self-contained and perhaps uneasy when a throng gathered round him, but that was long ago and far away.

Moving in public, stooping and talking into microphones, shaking hands with ranks of strangers, answering questions, posing for photographs, accepting that the throng would gaze at him as in a freak show, and carrying it all off smoothly – this was something Senna had been handling for a decade, sometimes on a daily basis, sometimes minute-by-minute. Betraying nervousness never had been a part. His self-possession was too rigid. He could bring charm, praise, anger, tears, indignation, vulnerability, desperate pity to the public gaze; but not nerves. You didn't see them and you wondered if they existed. Persons of a nervous disposition are not advised to try to exploit Formula 1 motor vehicles anyway. Certainly, O'Mahony attributes any suggestion of nerves to the fact that Senna wasn't *completely* comfortable in Italian (and by defini-tion might be asked questions with unfamiliar words in them about

BELOW LEFT Getting to know the Williams car, Estoril, January 1994 (Allsport).

BELOW Contemplating his new team, Estoril, January 1994 (Allsport).

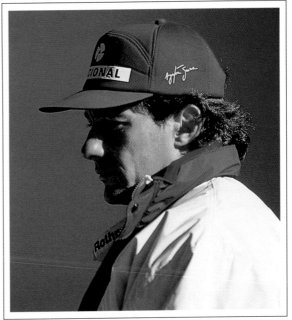

a mountain bike: the Formula 1 words he knew by heart and could mouth just like that). Against this must be put the thoughts of Pino Allievi, a leading Italian racing journalist, who insists that Senna spoke Italian *as well as any ordinary Italian*. Perhaps Assumpcao is nearer the mark: Senna wasn't nervous but just plain tired. Creating a business and simultaneously meeting the demands of Formula 1 was taking its toll. Sometimes he'd be up until 1.30am phoning Brazil.

However, a few days before this launch, Senna had telephoned his sister, Viviane Lalli, who has said "we talked for a long time. He was very low, though I will not say why."

The mystery of this endures, and will endure unless Lalli chooses to elaborate, but it surely cannot have been his personal life. He'd met and fallen in love with a 21-year-old model called Adriane Galisteu some 14 months before. The phrase *former model* suggests an exquisite hourglass with nothing between her ears, but no creature fitting this description could have interested Senna for long, if at all. Galisteu was a great deal more than that. If her account of their relationship is to be believed – and there is no reason not to, because she describes it with a soul-bearing, tenderised topsy-turvy authenticity which rings absolutely true – he was extremely happy to be in love with her. O'Mahony is convinced about that too, as we shall see. So are others. Senna would stay evasive about actual marriage (he had a divorce behind him in a previous life when he'd been no more than a kid, and caution in such a commitment was understandable) but that does not disturb the authenticity of the relationship or that one day soon, surely, marriage would become a probability. All else aside, he'd always talked of wanting children, always talked of what a fulfilling experience that would have to be, always made a fuss of children.

This Thursday, Galisteu would go to the Berlitz school in Sao Paulo to work on her English, something Senna insisted she do and for which he paid, albeit as a present to her. English, he knew, was the language you'd need in motor racing but also in the world outside, no matter where you went. She'd even sent him a saucy (well, sexy) fax one time in English to prove how much her command of the language had improved. On the morrow – the Friday – she'd board an overnight Varig flight to Lisbon and proceed to Senna's house in Faro. She'd watch the San Marino Grand Prix on television on the Sunday and await his return, which was estimated at 8.30pm. They would spend the European season – five months to the Grand Prix at Jerez in early September – together. She could hardly wait to see him again and, he'd said on the phone, he could hardly wait to see her. Ayrton Senna did not say such things carelessly.

It's tempting to conclude that he'd chosen Faro for a house because it was just about as near Brazil as he could get in Europe, and not just physically. They shared the same language (although, as Senna once explained to me, it's a bit like the difference between English-English and American-English: "we have some of our own special words"). Faro, Portugal, has a similar sort of climate to Brazil, similar sort of mentality maybe, sun-kissed people, stretch out and relax, don't fret about tomorrow. Faro was almost linked by an umbilical cord to his beloved Brazil, the only former colony in South America speaking Portuguese. Whoever you are, you feel most comfortable in your own language, no matter that Senna could also speak English, Spanish and, as we have seen, Italian. Faro offered space, which his apartment in Monte Carlo could never do: four or five bedrooms, a swimming pool and of course handy proximity to all the European races in his plane. There may have been even more pragmatic reasons, however. He could jog on the beach, a favourite way of keeping fit, and not be molested. In these surroundings – distant Faro, which had no connection to Formula 1 – those who wandered the beach weren't expecting to see him. There are tales of people saying *I thought I saw Ayrton Senna but I can't have done.*

As the mountain bike launch chugged along Senna appeared visibly to relax. If he was tired his physical and mental strength were overcoming that. Inevitably he had to field Formula 1 questions, specifically what he thought of his 1994 Championship chances. Thus far he'd spun off in Brazil trying to catch young Michael Schumacher in the Benetton, and been rudely rammed at the start of the Pacific Grand Prix at Aida, Japan. In starkest terms, Schumacher 20, Senna 0. That may partly be why he felt low. Imola, third race of the season, might well be pivotal. Schumacher, 10 years younger, was outdriving anything that tried to get near him. That had never happened to Ayrton Senna before. He'd been the one doing it to the others. The Williams car, overall unbeatable in 1992 and 1993, somehow didn't feel right to his touch and one time he wondered to Galisteu if he hadn't joined the team too late. Teams don't stay unbeatable for ever. It's a question of fine judgement. You can never be sure you've got the judgement right (and your opponents got it wrong) until it's too late. You've signed, you're in and that's it, no sanctuary.

> Sensible people spoke of him winning all 16 races

To compound Senna's immediate problems were three factors. The first stabbed the moment he departed Marlboro McLaren after six seasons to join Rothmans Williams Renault. He stirred profound anticipation. This had been raised by Nigel Mansell's amazing season with the Williams car in 1992 (108 points, his team-mate Riccardo Patrese next on 56), and Alain Prost's amazing season with the Williams car in 1993 (99 points, Senna next on 73). Clearly, Senna would paralyse 1994 and sensible people spoke of him winning *all 16* races; but, so far, Schumacher 20, Senna 0.

The second factor stabbed now because rumours suggested that some of the opposition were running barely legal cars. These, I stress, were rumours and are completely unproven but that doubt cannot have helped Senna's equilibrium. He faced a position where, overall, he might not be able to win the Championship whatever he did. He could milk and goad and cajole and scheme temporary advantages – as he'd done with Marlboro McLaren in 1993 – but an opponent with a decisively better car couldn't be withstood over the 16 races. Perhaps Senna felt low about that, about screwing so much out of himself, about risking his life and wringing so much out of so many other people preparing the car, but being ultimately helpless against Schumacher and Schumacher's Benetton. You do your best yet at day's end nothing remains except to submit. Senna spent his life without accepting submission, or *hating* it if he couldn't escape it. Defeat in single races could produce extreme reactions in him. When he made a mistake and crashed at Monaco in 1988 – he'd held a comfortable lead – he retreated to the sanctuary of his apartment and was still crying five hours later.

The third factor stabbed because the rules had been changed, banishing electronic driver aids on the cars and, as a consequence, making them more difficult to drive. Senna had spoken about this by saying *we'll be lucky if we get through the season without a big accident.* Many, many people returned to these words and found a meaning in them after Imola.

At the launch, someone raised the subject of illegality but Senna fended that off diplomatically. He could be consummately careful when he chose, every nuance, every comma in place and *whoever you are, you cannot misinterpret what I have said because I have selected the words with laboured precision. If you quote what I have said there will be no misinterpretation. If you twist the words that I have said, I can't control that and I'll live with the consequences. The way it is and the way it has always been — but I try to control it with my laboured precision. It's why I hesitate for so long before I answer the question. And anyway I want to say what I want to say.* After the launch he did about six television interviews, which was quite normal. They take their place among the thousands of others he gave — each wanting to know something, each want a part of him revealed now and to us.

From Padua, Senna took a helicopter with his 26-year-old brother Leonardo and two Carraro executives direct to the Imola circuit. O'Mahony, with Senna's business manager Julian Jakobi as a passenger, flew the HS125 to the little airport of Forli, south of Imola, a journey which O'Mahony says took "just under 20 minutes." The landing fees here were less than the big airport of Bologna. Why pay more if you don't have to? The plane would be parked there until Senna returned to it after the race and it would take him to Faro and Adriane.

The San Marino Grand Prix is a misnomer. The race, at the very Italian town of Imola, is really nowhere near the tiny, mountainous 'republic' and precious few Formula 1 people have ever bothered or enjoyed the leisure to go there (Senna had *raced* there).

Senna might have flown with O'Mahony and gone straight to his hotel, but no such easy option ever suited him. He wanted to see what the team were doing with the „ar (which had been undergoing fairly fundamental aerodynamic changes since Aida, itself a reason to go and have a look; not that he needed a reason).

We have reached the gathering, the curious preparatory ritual enacted before each race. Formula 1 teams don't just arrive, they set up camp long before the transporters come in.

Consider the scale of it. Williams need two transporters, one loaded with three cars (Senna's, Hill's, and the spare), the other a cavern of spares and electrical wizardry. These transporters will leave the factory at Didcot, near London, on the Monday, aiming to be in place at Imola on the Wednesday. Simultaneously, Renault transporters will be heading south from France with some 15 engines. From the English Midlands, six Goodyear transporters will be going there too, with 2,500 tyres for the teams (cost of each tyre, $600). Invariably the mechanics – who fly – get weaving when they come in on the Thursday, and they create an increasing tempo because the cars must be absolutely ready for the first session on the Friday, the morning free practice. If Formula 1 is habitually serious about itself, it starts to get much more serious about itself now. This is not *it*, but a countdown has begun, the minutes melting towards the free practice.

Throughout his career Ayrton Senna had taken a profound interest in the preparation of his car. Once upon a time you'd rarely see a driver on the Thursday except Senna, who was probing, asking, examining, staying until nightfall. What you'd glimpse was a slender chap deep in the pit, nothing unusual, situation normal, and you'd walk on. These days his arrival at a circuit loomed as an event in itself and, when he did arrive, the whole pace in pits and paddock quickened, the throng gathered. Alone, and by his presence, he could fill the emptiness of the Thursday. *He's here . . .*

This Thursday he spent a few moments with the mechanics and also spoke to Richard West, the Williams Director of Marketing. They knew each other well. Senna wanted to be told how much promotional activity he would be committed to, an important matter over any Grand Prix weekend and a delicate one. Someone as experienced as West would strike the correct balance between satisfying sponsors and guests – who would be making demands on Senna – and creating necessary space for Senna to exist in peace, concentrate on the driving, the real reason he was there. The rest was needed to make the big wheel turn. The way it is. Senna also spoke to Assumpcao who had the unceasing and onerous task of controlling journalistic access to him: she had to draw her own balance between trying to make him available and trying to prevent him from being over-run.

At any Grand Prix each moment is valuable and often at Senna's level accounted for in advance. The basic format is struck in stone, regardless of climates or continents or cultures. There is the free practice on the Friday morning followed by the first qualifying session (1.0 to 2.0), same on the Saturday, with the big temperature-rise on the Sunday: the morning warm-up and the race early afternoon. Each session (apart from the race) is followed by a lengthy debrief. Cumulatively it leaves very few of those valuable moments when the driver does interviews, has his photograph taken, signs things for little Johnny, chats to whoever the sponsor has brought and, in the case of Hill and Senna, treats the Williams guests to a verbal lap of the circuit after the drivers' briefing on race morning. Moreover, adding to this, Senna would constantly be moving through the throng which roved and lurked and tracked him, every step he took.

The talk with West over, Senna took a Renault Espace to Castel San Pietro nine kilometres from Imola. Renault have a fleet of cars at the disposal of team personnel and, understandably, are not anxious for team personnel to be seen in anything else. He went first to the Romagnola restaurant, a plain but wholesome establishment with a marble plaque on the outside wall near the door. It says:

In this house was born on the 15th of March 1839 Battista Acquaderni who died in Bologna in 1922. He was one of the founders of the Italian Catholic Youth Organisation. This man, with his word and his example, called the younger generation to the faith.

Senna booked a table for 8.30pm. He'd eaten at the Romagnola regularly since 1991. That year the hotel where he stayed, the Castello, had phoned and said "can you keep a table for Senna?" The Liverani family who ran the restaurant thought *Senna! Oh my God!* He arrived with a beautiful blonde and asked only to eat in peace. The Romagnola had an advantage: a small dining room as well as a larger one. They could put him in the smaller one and not let anybody else in. They didn't serve him anything sophisticated. At the end of the meal the family asked Senna if he really was Senna and he said *yes!* They asked for an autograph and proffered a block note-book. He signed every sheet. The family sensed that the tranquillity appealed to him; and so he came back. One of the family says that Senna was "so rich he could have *bought* the San Domenico restaurant, one of the most expensive in the whole area, but instead he loved the simple things."

Now, this Thursday, Senna made a fuss of the family and said how pleased he was to see them again. The table booked, he drove out of Castel San Pietro along a winding, descending road – a beautiful valley spread before him, the sort of softening panorama Italy suddenly offers you like a vision – to the hotel Castello, an L-shaped building set in rolling countryside. He'd stayed there every year since 1989. Frank Williams stayed there too, and so did Senna's old boss at Marlboro McLaren, Ron Dennis. Senna walked past the wishing well in the foyer: a carved stone base with a wrought-iron canopy arched over it and into which residents threw coins so that they'd have the good luck to return some time for another stay at the hotel. He went to the reception desk and enacted a familiar ritual. He wrote on a piece of paper a list of people he'd accept telephone calls from. Any other calls for him would be fielded by the reception, noted and given to him whenever he came to collect his room key or surrendered it going out. He could scan the notes and return the calls or not, as he wished.

> He wrote on a piece of paper a list of people he'd accept calls from

Because Senna had stayed at the Castello so long the word had spread that he'd be there. Bouquets arrived early for him, mainly roses from female admirers. The staff arranged these in his room. He rarely tarried at the reception because people were drawn to the hotel for a peek at him, an ogle at him, a vision of the real living image of him, an autograph, a photo with him; and there was only so much he could give of himself every valuable moment of every day. He took the lift nearby to the second floor. He always had the same suite, number 200, and he had that again: a small hallway, a bedroom with a TV and a curious painting above the bed-head – four Chinese-looking landscapes – a bathroom, a sitting room with another TV and sofa and chairs in day-glo purple. It cost 400,000 lira (£150) per night and was pleasant rather than extravagant. From the window he could see indoor and outdoor swimming pools and the rolling countryside.

Frank Williams had the suite below, number 100, and Ron Dennis the one above, number 300.

Ann Bradshaw of Williams explains that "the whole team doesn't stay in the same hotel. They tend to be scattered all over the place" – governed not just by cost but the availability of rooms. O'Mahony, as an example, stayed elsewhere and so did Assumpcao.

The driver naturally wants as few uncertainties as possible. Senna knew the hotel, liked his room, knew the man running it – Valentino Torsini – and the Romagnola was just up the hill, its private room giving sanctuary.

With him this weekend were those genuinely close to him (which many claimed to be and few were): Leonardo, Carlos Braga (a banker and an absolutely dependable friend from way back), Jakobi, Galvao Bueno (who worked for TV Globo, the Brazilian channel which covered the races), Celso Lemos (who managed Senna Licensing in Brazil), Ubirajara Guimaraes (who managed Senna Imports), and the masseur Josef Leberer. It was a larger party than usual for Senna. Ordinarily there'd be only Jakobi, Leberer and of course O'Mahony and Assumpcao.

The advantage of the small room in the Romagnola was more than privacy. It was large enough to put the tables together and accommodate whatever entourage Senna brought. This Thursday, that was himself and six others. He wore casual-chic, which he liked: smart jeans, shirt, maybe a pullover slung over his shoulders. He left before 10pm, booking again for the following evening, which he always did. Andrew Longmore writes that "he rarely went to bed before midnight but was a notoriously late riser." (In Senna's Formula Ford 2000 days in England in 1982, his manager Dennis Rushen described him as typically South American, "didn't want to get out of bed.") Senna was careful about what he ate and this is one of his daily menus, structured by Leberer.

BREAKFAST
Muesli, lots of fresh berries and yoghurt
Fruit tea
Multi-grain bread with strawberry jam

MID-MORNING
Carrot, orange and honey drink made of fresh ingredients

LUNCH
Fresh salad of tomato, basil, lettuce and avocado
Grilled chicken with fresh pasta and fresh tomato sauce
Fresh fruit salad
Water

DINNER
Grilled salmon with fresh green vegetable risotto
Fruit of fresh berries
Water

A note at the bottom instructed *Always use fresh produce, olive oil for cooking and fresh herbs. Use honey instead of sugar for sweetener.*

He drove to the circuit on the Friday morning and, in the light of what would happen there, the lay-out will help. You enter the circuit and turn into a broad, long paddock. To one side, a dozen or more motorhomes are parked side by side butting onto the perimeter wall. Each team has one: the sanctuary. To the other side there's a tall, imposing control tower which joins the main building. Its ground floor is divided into the pits, its upper floors contain offices, a restaurant, hospitality suites and the Media Centre. This building faces the grid and a grandstand the far side of the track. To it come the teams' transporters which, side by side, nestle into the back of the pits, disgorging the cars, spares and equipment. The paddock is broad enough to allow a walkway between the motorhomes and the transporters, but that's generally choked by mechanics wheeling tyres on trolleys, guests ambling about, friends chatting, team personnel who move compulsively, camera crews on the look-out, not counting a hundred journalists also on the look-out and maybe, just maybe, a driver cutting a course to somewhere. There are cables underfoot, little generators which hum, machinery, plates of sandwiches being ferried, movement, movement. The choking activity somehow lends a sense of urgency and purpose. Down from the main building stands the Medical Centre: a low, white building with a helipad next to it and a protective mesh screen in front of it.

The track itself uncoils from the grid and keeps on coiling and uncoiling for 3.132 miles (5.05 kilometres): it curves hard-left (Tamburello), straightens, kinks right (Villeneuve), twists left (Tosa), flows left (Piratella), stabs right-left-right (Acque Minerale), straightens a bit to a left-right stab (Varianta Alta), straightens to a hard-loop (Rivazza), straightens briefly to a fast right-left (Variante Bassa) which pitches the driver along a mini-straight into the 90-degree left-right (Traguardo) and the start-finish line in front of the pits, the main building and the grandstand. The Medical Centre is virtually level with Traguardo.

In the Friday morning practice session, the weather hot and dry, Senna did 22 laps and expressed himself satisfied with the aerodynamic changes made to the car since Aida, and these changes were visible when the car turned in to the corners. Senna was quickest with one minute 21.598 seconds, Hill over a second slower, Schumacher third.

The temperature had risen to 27 degrees when first qualifying began. The Austrian Karl Wendlinger in a Sauber emerged almost immediately, then Heinz-Harald Frentzen in the other Sauber, then Gianni Morbidelli in the Footwork. The potential pole men bided their time, calculated their moment. Schumacher was the first of them and, using the full width of the track, warmed to 1:22.564. As Schumacher travelled round the back of the circuit, Senna came out, the Williams "bottoming" and shedding yellow sparks through Tamburello. In the pits Frank Williams watched intently on the TV monitor and saw Senna's helmet bounce-stutter-bounce as the car ran across Imola's bumps. Senna thrust in 1:22.430. As Senna travelled into his second flying lap, virtually as he placed the Williams safely near the inside kerb at Tamburello and went crisply and cleanly round, his young Brazilian protege Rubens Barrichello came hard through Rivazza in his Jordan. The car missed the apex of the next right-left, Barrichello dug smoke from the rear tyres under reflex braking and tried to straighten it. He couldn't and the car rushed the far kerbing. The slope of that kerbing launched the car sideways across a tight segment of grass and it brushed the top of the tyre wall, battered the metal fencing above. It landed savaged and on its side. This looked dreadful.

Professor Sid Watkins, Formula 1's resident travelling doctor and a man totally trusted, was there in a matter of moments. The car had been righted by marshals but Barrichello remained in the cockpit. It was just after 1.14. The red flags were hoisted immediately. Senna, touring in, did not see the accident but could not have failed to see the aftermath. He had to pass it to regain the pits.

Within five minutes Barrichello had been taken to the Medical Centre, very close to the scene of his accident. Assumpcao went to the Jordan pit for news because she wanted to know herself and she knew Senna would want to know, too. Senna himself went to the Medical Centre. On the way there he passed the rear of the

Jordan pit where he met Brian Hart, who made the engines which Jordan used – and had made the engines which the Toleman team used when Senna entered Formula 1 in 1984. "How is Rubens?" Senna asked urgently. Hart remembers that Senna looked "very shocked". Hart had seen the accident on a TV monitor and knew how bad it looked. He was able to reassure Senna, however, that Barrichello had hurt his nose but otherwise seemed fine. "I'm going to see him," Senna said, and strode on. One report (Longmore) suggests that Senna found "the front door of the Medical Centre blocked, and vaulted a fence to get in the back." This appears unlikely because Professor Watkins had no objection to him visiting Barrichello and permitted it. "Rubens was all right so I let him in."

Barrichello was quoted – and the words went straight round the world – as saying that when he regained consciousness "the first face I saw was Ayrton's. He had tears in his eyes, like the accident had been his own. I had never seen that before." Today, reflecting as best he can (he had been unconscious, don't forget), Barrichello says "I remember him being the first person I saw. I remember him saying that I was OK, just to keep calm. I don't know if he was crying, I can't remember. I read afterwards that he was speaking to someone on the telephone and crying but at that stage . . . I can't remember. He didn't say much to me because I was going to be put in a helicopter to the hospital."

Satisfied that Barrichello had suffered no more than slight injuries ("I'm off to play with the nurses and I'll be back tomorrow," Barrichello quipped later), Senna walked to the pits. Even on this short journey along the paddock the throng of some 30 to 40 pursued and hemmed him. Two hand-held television cameras probed, almost leering at his face as cameras do in close up. *Show us every bead of sweat, every eye movement, every discomfort. We're getting live history, you know, as it happens and you* – the viewer – *are getting it, too.*

The session resumed at 1.40 and Senna got back in the car, went for it. "I don't feel that I ever drove the car properly. After the acci-

Senna and Nicola Larini (Ferrari) after the crash at Aida.

dent of Rubens I wasn't driving well — not consistent, not able to do it properly. It was just myself not being able to concentrate." That did not prevent him recording 1:21.548, provisional pole from Schumacher on 1:22.015.

This is the sequence of events. When the accident stopped the session, Senna had been third fastest. Now he worked through a lap of 1:24.067, conservative and obviously so. He stayed away from the kerbs. On his second lap he did use the kerbs, urging the Williams much, much harder: 1:21.837 and provisional pole. Then he spun — the car reduced to a slewed standstill — but he churned it and set off again, furious wheel spin, smoke from the rears, a swathe of rubber marking the path the car took. That was 40 minutes into the session. Senna returned to the pits. He emerged onto the track with some three and a half minutes of the session remaining and urged the Williams harder still: 1:21.548. By then, Barrichello had been flown by helicopter to the Maggiore Hospital in Bologna for tests.

After the session, Senna was emotionally and physically exhausted; almost irritated by some supporters in the main building above the pits who bayed their encouragement and told him he'd got the beating of Schumacher. He wasn't in the mood to hear combative calls like these. Reportedly, he attempted to do a brief interview with a television reporter over Barrichello but couldn't. He tried to speak the same sentence three times, made his excuses and vanished into one of the Williams transporters, forbidden to all but team personnel. Sanctuary. He stayed there for half an hour and when he did come out he was able to talk, about his lack of concentration, about how "chaotic" the whole session felt, and to a knot of Italian journalists he stressed how dangerous parts of the circuit were.

He walked to the motorhome and moved into a profound discussion with his engineer, David Brown, because Senna felt (as it emerged later, and in the words of another) there was "a big engineering problem with the car." Brown went briefly away and Senna came out to give

The aftermath, Aida (Empics).

a group of journalists a promised interview about his business empire. This took place in the seating area butting on to the motorhome. One of the journalists, Mark Fogarty of *Carweek*, estimated Senna answered questions for between 15 and 20 minutes but with the caveat that as soon as Brown returned the de-brief would resume. Fogarty was struck by how Senna appeared – "extremely tired, eyes red and glassy. Drawn." Fogarty was also struck by the difficulty Senna had in concentrating on his answers.

Senna was famous for the care he took in this. He weighed his answers for a long time (I once timed him at 13 seconds) because he rehearsed and chose his words exactly. *Whoever you are, you cannot misinterpret what I have said.* However, Fogarty noticed that the gap between questions and answers became even longer than normal and those answers were "halting," as if Senna was trying to regain his concentration rather than selecting from his vocabulary: a powerful difference in a man accustomed to the mechanisms of absolute concentration on the topic in hand to the exclusion of all else.

Brown returned and Senna departed to the upper deck of the motorhome to resume the de-brief, wrestle with the engineering problem. He came back an hour later and told the journalists he wasn't in the mood to continue the interrupted interview but would do so on the morrow after second qualifying. The journalists drifted off. Assumpcao went to the Maggiore to see Barrichello.

Senna left the circuit around 8.0 and dined at the Romagnola with, among others, Bueno of TV Globo. Evidently Senna was between two moods. He asked Bueno how Barrichello was, reflecting his continued anxiety, and when Bueno couldn't give him the latest bulletin ribbed him gently about being a newsman who didn't have up-to-the-minute information. The Liveranis remember Senna's mood as "black." That night, too, in the hotel he and some of the support team sat round a table and Senna talked for a long time about chance, about the meaning and consequences of chance. He appeared still preoccupied by Barrichello's accident and started to mention launching safety initiatives before the next Grand Prix, at Monaco in two weeks. He went to his room shortly after 11pm. While he slept, Galisteu took off from Sao Paulo for Lisbon at 10.10 local time – 1.10am in Europe.

Seen in isolation, the impact which Barrichello's crash exercised on Senna appears difficult to comprehend, no matter that Barrichello was a Brazilian, a protege and, at 22, represented the future. Barrichello had survived intact, Barrichello was chirpy. It turned out to be just another crash, just another confirmation that Formula 1 cars were so robust they'd take wild batterings and cocoon the driver from the most extreme consequences. No man had died during a Grand Prix meeting for 12 years and no man had died in a Formula 1 car for eight years.

Questions arise, and I don't think we'll ever know the answers.

Did Senna, perceptive as he was, sense that *whatever anybody claimed for the cars* Formula 1 had been very, very lucky across – respectively – the 12 years and eight, and that one day the luck wouldn't hold? That could easily have been today, Friday, 29 April 1994.

Did the accumulation of pressures – Schumacher strong, Imola pivotal, the engineering problem with the car, the rule changes, all of it, all of it – heighten his senses to an extent that something shockingly unexpected like the crash of the protege was damn near too much? Of course, Senna had been under pressure before – every Formula 1 driver is – but not, perhaps, this peculiar and pervading conjunction of pressures. To break down and cry in a Medical Centre when you are looking at a driver who is OK and who, moreover, is poised to make quips about chasing nurses, represents a strange reaction. This was particularly true for Senna who'd seen dreadful crashes before (the worst to Martin Donnelly, Gerhard Berger and Derek Warwick), had driven since the age of four, had inhabited Formula 1 for a decade and was into his 161st Grand Prix meeting.

Did the absence of Alain Prost, who retired at the end of 1993, increase the pressure in a subtle way? Throughout his Formula 1 career, in testing, qualifying and the races, Senna had had a benchmark to measure against – Prost. Now (and begging Schumacher's pardon) Senna represented the only benchmark, and might have felt that each time he drove he was driving into the unknown, no comparisons valid. You see this for what it is. *If Prost can do that time, I can screw enough from myself and the car to beat it.* Without the comparison, how did Senna know how much he must turn the screw?

> Senna had never faced the realities of his own profession so starkly before

"Ayrton was shaken, he was very much shaken," O'Mahony says. "He was a mentor to Barrichello." O'Mahony accepts that it still shook Senna much more than you'd have expected, accepts that this was strange.

On the Saturday, arm in plaster, Barrichello returned to the circuit and remained chirpy. "You OK, you OK?" Senna asked him. Barrichello talked about driving again as soon as possible. "Don't be a fool," Senna said. "You think you are OK but you might not be. I know from some of my own accidents." (Barrichello remembers Senna saying to him "take your time", and adds "I understood. I did take my time, I had two weeks without driving, then I came to England to test.")

The morning free practice passed, superficially, in the most ordinary way but during it Senna did something extremely uncharacteristic.

O'Mahony stood in the back of the pits, and hereby hangs the tale which still makes O'Mahony wonder. "Uncanny," is his description. Before we get to that, another tale. "I didn't have a pass for the pits," O'Mahony says. "I was in the paddock behind but I wasn't actually allowed into the pits without one. This 6ft, 13-stone Italian 'heavy' (Imola abounds with official bouncers to try and keep control) stopped me and Ayrton saw it. He came over and said to the guy 'they're with me'. So there was no problem, we just walked in. As a result of that the guy let us in all day because he recognised who we were." Now the uncanny part. O'Mahony had worked for Senna, flying the plane, for three years and during that time – although he wanted a photograph of himself with Senna – he didn't have one. "I thought it was a bit *naff* of me to ask him. I didn't really want to ask him." Understandably so. O'Mahony was a very experienced pilot who'd flown heads of state, was old enough to be Senna's father and, anyway, Senna employed him. Senna was aware that O'Mahony wanted a photograph.

O'Mahony stood in the back of the pits because "I aimed to be unobtrusive so if he wanted things I was there but I wasn't getting in the way. If he did want something he'd come over and ask 'Owen, could you go and do so-and-so for me?' The trick was to remain out of the way but be there. During a Grand Prix weekend, he was single-minded, tunnel vision. Now he got out of the car, took his helmet off and – it was most unlike him because we never talked during sessions – he said 'Owen, I've got the photos for you'. And he produced two photos.

"One was of him flying the aeroplane for the first time, and which I had taken with a fish-eye lens. We were approaching Faro after a Grand Prix, it was at night and he had a nice wry smile. By the time I'd given the camera back I thought we were too high so I had to go round again before we landed. He signed it *To Owen, that's why we missed the direct approach to Faro.*

"The second photo was on the pit lane wall at Imola and I didn't know it was being taken, just he and I talking and smiling. Nobody else around, a lovely photograph. Someone had taken it the day before and he'd remembered. It was odd. In a sense, a photographer had taken it completely by chance (in the context of O'Mahony wanting just such a photograph and happening to be with Senna on the pit lane wall) and Ayrton hadn't forgotten. He signed it *To Owen with best wishes*. It was out of character for him to think about anything but racing during a racing session, it was almost as if he wanted to tie up some loose ends."

Galisteu landed at Lisbon at midday and travelled to Sintra, 30 kilometres from the airport, where she would spend the afternoon at the home of Luiza and Carlos de Almeida Braga – a favoured visiting-place of Senna's, and where he had often stayed. Carlos Braga, of course, was at Imola. That evening Galisteu would fly on to Faro.

At 1.0 the second session for the grid began. At 1.18 Senna prepared to make his first run but, before that, he watched what the others were doing on a TV monitor in the pits. He saw live coverage of the Austrian Roland Ratzenberger, a rookie in a Simtek, go off at the Villeneuve curve at 200mph and smash into the concrete wall. Senna sensed instantly that the luck no longer held. He retreated to the rear of the pit and covered his face with his hands, then walked down the pit lane and commandeered an official car to take him to the crash. When he reached it, Ratzenberger was en route to the Medical Centre but the wreckage of the Simtek and its distribution told Senna everything.

He returned to the pits in the official car and walked to the Medical Centre. This time Professor Watkins would not allow him in. "Even when Mansell tried to get in after Berger's accident (at Tamburello, 1989) he was turned away because, you know, everybody's busy and the scene can be a bit of a surprise to someone who's not been in an intensive care unit before. If they are sensitive, then I'd prefer them not to see it. He arrived at the door as I happened to be walking out and I guided him away, whereas the day before Rubens was all right so I let him in."

Ratzenberger was only clinically alive.

Watkins remembers that Senna was "very shocked. He had never faced the reality of his profession before so starkly, because no-one had been killed during his time in Formula 1 (at a Grand Prix). He was always fatalistic about death. He was a religious man and intelligent enough to think it through. This was the first time it had come so close. He was very quiet, but he remained resolute, not questioning out loud the meaning of his sport or his own position." This conversation took place on some grass, Senna arms folded, Watkins with his hands on his hips.

"Was there something troubling Senna even before the accidents? I think he was genuinely worried about safety," Watkins says, "and that was starting to preoccupy him. Mind you, it's a sign of maturity. I think he was missing McLaren, too. You've to remember it was his 'family' there, wasn't it? So the whole season was very different for him: he'd gone to a new team, he'd had two unsuccessful races, one getting shunted off at Aida and in Brazil he lost it – didn't he? – lost control of the car in the dry . . ."

While Senna and Watkins spoke, Martin Whitaker, Press Delegate of the FIA, waited nearby. He, too, had gone to the Medical Centre for news of Ratzenberger but clearly wouldn't intrude on the intensity of the interflow between Senna and Watkins. "When they had finished," Whitaker says, "I asked Senna if he knew what had happened. He didn't reply. He just looked at me and walked away. I won't forget that look. To say it was fear would be over the top. He was just very worried. There was something different about him."

Neither Hill nor Senna took part in this second session. From the Medical Centre, Senna walked to the pits and discreetly in a corner informed Hill and Patrick Head that Ratzenberger was dead in all but name. Frank Williams gave him the choice of continuing or not, which was the only prudent course to take. If Senna felt a need to get into the car immediately – some drivers do – as personal therapy, Frank Williams would not deny him that. If Senna felt a need to distance himself from it and reflect, Frank Williams would not deny him that, either. They are all human beings, never claimed to be more or less.

Ratzenberger was flown to the Maggiore Hospital. The second session for the grid resumed at 2.05, while the helicopter bearing Ratzenberger approached the hospital. He arrived there at 2.08 and was officially pronounced dead at 2.15.

Senna walked to the Williams motorhome and changed from his driving overalls. He telephoned Galisteu in Sintra. She has estimated that the call lasted some 15 minutes and consisted of "sobs, complaints, doubts." She has written that he "really lost control" and said he didn't want to race on the Sunday. Nobody had ever heard him say anything like that before. She also records this fragment of their conversation.

Galisteu: "What? Isn't there going to be a race?"

Senna: "Don't you know them?"

That demands dissection because it carries such implications. Only one Grand Prix in modern times has been cancelled when the fraternity reached the circuit, Spa, 1985. The relaid surface of the track crumbled to the point where you could lift chunks of it with your hand. Senna was a newcomer to Spa then because the 1984 Belgian Grand Prix – his first year in Formula 1 – was run at Zolder. At Spa he'd spent the Wednesday roaming and jogging the circuit's entire length of 6.940 kilometres (4.312 miles) to memorise it, feel out the racing lines. Legend insists that, as the track worsened during second qualifying, Senna was so eager to drive he went out despite someone – not a member of his Lotus team – insisting "Ayrton, if I could order you not to go out I would, but I can't." In fact, Senna said after this second qualifying: "Believe me, there is no way we can run. First, you cannot really race when conditions are like this. Second, you have to drive off the line everywhere and you're going over marbles, not asphalt (marbles are slippery globules of rubber shed by tyres). You're going 20 seconds slower and risking 10 times more. There is nothing to be done. The race will have to be cancelled." However impetuous Senna was then, however eager, however much he cherished every minute in a car, he talked plain common sense. Spa was undriveable, even to him.

There is a very important difference between that and a fatality. When Gilles Villeneuve was killed in second qualifying for the Belgian Grand Prix at Zolder in 1982, the race went ahead. When Ricardo Paletti crashed at the start of the Canadian Grand Prix a month later – and was helicoptered to hospital, pronounced dead there much like Ratzenberger – the race restarted for its full 70 laps. Senna was without question aware of this: he had been at Zolder, driving Formula Ford

2000, and – studying Formula 1 carefully, as ambitious drivers do – cannot have avoided knowing about Canada. In its day, nobody avoided knowing about it.

ABOVE LEFT Part of the future was wheels, different wheels.

ABOVE The plaque outside the Romagnola restaurant (author).

And then there had been the accidents during Senna's own Formula 1 career, notably Berger at Tamburello in 1989, the Ferrari exploding in fire. The Imola race had been stopped to rescue Berger but subsequently re-started. Donnelly was massively mauled in first qualifying at Jerez in 1990, but second qualifying and the race went ahead quite normally.

The last man to die in a Formula 1 car before Ratzenberger was Elio de Angelis, testing a Brabham at the Paul Ricard circuit on 15 May 1986. Ten days later the Belgian Grand Prix took place at Spa, and however sombre the mood (which it certainly was) the race went ahead quite normally.

Outsiders may see this as callous, and cynics do point to the imperative of television ratings and the fact that television channels all over the world have scheduled the race; hence cancellation is a very big step and regular cancellation might call the whole thing into question. That is only one aspect. Every sane insider goes to every race knowing that something dreadful can take place there. Unless the insider finds a way of accepting this, accommodating it, he'd better stay home. That is absolutely essential to the driver because he is offering his own mortality against his desire; but whatever protective barriers he erects in his mind, whatever accommodations he reaches with his inner self, they can be stripped away very, very quickly when the dreadful does take place.

On Saturday, 30 April 1994, that is what happened to Gerhard Berger, who went to the Ferrari motorhome and "all my body was shaking." Berger began to erect his barriers again, asking himself if he would continue his career or end it instantly.

Once he answered this most personal of questions he returned to the pits and drove when the second qualifying session resumed.

On Saturday, 30 April 1994, that is what happened to Ayrton Senna and he reacted in a different way to Berger. He declined the offer of Frank Williams to drive again if he wished. He returned to the motorhome. Damon Hill and Damon's wife Georgina were there and Assumpcao came in. She found Senna's spirits "so low. I just stroked his head, talked to him a little, but he was very quiet." She had never touched him like that. They had touched before, but only in conversation and in the natural Brazilian way, to emphasise a point, celebrate a joke, maybe.

When the qualifying session ended, no competitor bettered Senna's Friday time. He would start the San Marino Grand Prix from pole position. Under FIA rules he was obliged to attend the post-session Press Conference and, in normal times – as Martin Whitaker points out – "it's a fineable offence if you don't." In this case, normality had gone. One of Ann Bradshaw's tasks as Williams PR lady was to remind her drivers they were expected at mandatory Press Conferences. She went to the motorhome and diplomatically asked Senna. "Absolutely not," Senna said. Frank Williams concurred. "Absolutely no way," Williams said and added that if there was any question of a fine the team would simply pay it.

Bradshaw made her way to the Media Centre and Maria Bellanca, doing a similar task for Benetton, was there and said Schumacher wouldn't be attending either. Bradshaw explained the situation to Whitaker who in turn explained to her that the Press Conference had been cancelled, the drivers weren't expected and it really wasn't a problem. Bradshaw concluded that the people running it "had hearts and they showed them." Berger, however – there by virtue of being third quickest – did give a Press Conference but only because he wanted to explain why he'd gone out again after Ratzenberger's crash. It had nothing to do with how or why he'd qualified third. Meanwhile Whitaker must, by the nature of his job, give an official communique to the media. Official communiques tend to be rigid and formalised, but within that structure Whitaker put it together as sensitively as he could.

The drivers required for the Pole Position Conference on Saturday, April 30th were Ayrton Senna, Michael Schumacher and Gerhard Berger.
Each driver was told of his requirement to attend the Pole Position Conference, either directly or through his team manager. In the event only Gerhard Berger attended the conference.
Due to the circumstances and the mood of both the teams and the media I would like to think that no further action be taken against the drivers Ayrton Senna and Michael Schumacher for not making themselves available.

No action was taken.

Around 3.0, the race Stewards summoned Senna from the motorhome about his taking the official car to Ratzenberger's accident. John Corsmit, an experienced official, was "a consultant to the Stewards. The meeting was in the Stewards' Office on the first floor of the control building. I was there, three Stewards, Senna and someone else (Whitaker). We asked exactly what had happened and we told him 'you cannot take a car from one of the officials without asking permission from the race control, you cannot go out on the track just like that when a session has been stopped under a red flag without permission. If somebody goes out onto the track, we want to know who is going where'. In fact, I said to Senna 'even for you, it must be very easy just to knock on the door and ask if you can go there'." (Corsmit feels, reflecting, that no Italian official in an official car would dare refuse that car to the great Ayrton Senna if Senna suddenly wanted to commandeer it. They are all human beings.)

Whitaker was "there when the Stewards talked to Ayrton and sure he was very, very low. Quite naturally so. Corsmit is a firm man but I'll tell you something. He was a bomber pilot during the war, he's seen plenty of situations which are emotionally charged and he's not a fool. He's a compassionate guy – and he has to be – to do the job he's doing. He's not oblivious to, or unaware of, the emotions of people and that was particularly true with Senna. They were very close to each other in many ways. Yes, of course, Corsmit and the Stewards did realise that Senna felt concerned. What they said was 'yes, we understand this and we understand your desire to have a look and be aware of what is happening and so forth, but if you want to do it again please inform us and we'll give you the assistance to do it. Please don't just go and commandeer a car'."

One report suggests Senna felt such distress he shouted towards Corsmit "at least someone is concerned about safety." Corsmit doesn't recall this and neither does Whitaker. "I can't remember whether he got angry or not," Corsmit says, "but he was not happy with the situation, the whole situation. I don't know whether he was himself or not himself, but I do know he was not happy with what we were talking about. Maybe he shouted at me. I don't know. I had never had problems with him before. Well, what am I saying, problems? Of course, we all know about the situation we had had two times with Alain Prost at Suzuka (Prost and Senna crashed there in 1989 and 1990) and with Senna and Prost one time at Hockenheim (Prost claimed Senna weaved at him and forced him off the circuit in 1991).

> At these speeds our reactions and our sensations are at the limit

"Senna and I had spoken to each other a lot over the years but that does not mean we were adversaries. No, never adversaries. I got on very well with Senna and, normally speaking, I had no problems at all. I think he was the best driver that we ever had. Shouting at me? He never did that. When the meeting was over, Senna just went away. There was no reprimand, no anything. We could have reprimanded him, oh yes, but the (whole) situation was bad enough for the Stewards not to do anything about it: just to let him know that he couldn't do things like that. It was the last time I spoke to him."

Whitaker says "I can imagine the meeting could become highly-charged, but there was a point where I went out of the room. Whilst as FIA Press Delegate I am in a privileged position of being allowed in there, obviously I can't influence anything. If things get a bit awkward I leave and then, if a story leaks to the journalists, people can't say I abused the privilege and leaked it." Senna's anger may have revolved around the fact that he – Senna – was sure it was a *Steward's* car he had commandeered and thus his action was de facto sanctioned.

Senna returned to the motorhome and remained there, alone, until 5.30. He emerged wearing his white *Senninha* tee-shirt, face drawn, to go to the hotel. He told a handful of journalists that at these speeds "our reactions and our sensations are at the limit. We cannot control all the parameters of the car. I fear for the young drivers: the speeds on the circuits are higher and nothing's done about it." He literally bumped into Mike Fogarty of *Carweek*, remembered the truncated interview of yesterday, murmured "I don't want to talk about anything but ring me during the week and we'll do it over the phone," and was gone.

Assumpcao had worked for Senna for five years. She hadn't been a motor racing fan nor, in a sense, had she become one. This was her job. The death of Ratzenberger hit her very hard, so hard that she couldn't eat, so she lingered at the circuit. At around 7.0 Frank Williams asked her "how's Ayrton? Is he OK? I want to know." She explained that he was going out to dine with friends. That reassured Williams who said "I was afraid he might be on his own."

When Senna arrived at the hotel a wedding reception was under way in the restaurant and immediately Senna was recognised. He agreed to pose for a picture or two with the bride and groom. Whatever his feelings about Ratzenberger, whatever his state of mind, he carried this task off.

He did have an obligation that evening. It was Josef Leberer's birthday and Senna and other members of the support team dined with Leberer at the Romagnola. Senna arrived at 7.0 and ate very little. Jakobi has described this dinner as "a sombre affair" and during it Senna asked Leberer, an Austrian, all about what kind of a person Ratzenberger had been. Ratzenberger was new to Formula 1 in 1994, hadn't qualified for the race in Brazil but finished eleventh in Aida. The way Formula 1 is, Ratzenberger was almost a complete stranger. The Liveranis heard the talk passing to and fro, heard it move to safety, to improving safety in the pit lane – Senna recounting that one time a Tyrrell had nearly crashed him in the pit lane. One of the Liveranis says that "all evening he seemed preoccupied, very worried, much shocked." He ate spaghetti with plain tomatoes on it and they'd prepared a special little salad but it was too salty for him. Great consternation. They hastened to make another. He drank only mineral water, as always: sparkling and at room temperature.

Shortly before he left at around 9.0 word came that Castel San Pietro's police were expressing a lively interest in the Renault car parked illegally outside the restaurant. Much further consternation, followed by a physical outpouring of Liveranis who explained *it's Ayrton Senna's car and he's going in a moment*. You see the way it is in Italy: the police would surely have *guarded* the car to keep it safe for him and parking tickets are strictly for the birds; but anyway Senna was going soon. He shook hands with the Liveranis and they thought he was more relaxed again, quiet like usual, returning towards his old self. He said "thank you, I'll see you next year."

Senna returned to the hotel and the receptionist gave him a message from Frank Williams to *please come up to my room for a talk*. Senna went there and had calmed considerably. He said he would race. A little while later, Jakobi bumped into Senna who was standing outside the door to his – Senna's – room wearing pyjamas with the white tee-shirt over them.

"Ayrton, you're dressed funnily," Jakobi said.

"That's probably true," Senna murmured and summoned a flicker of a smile. "I've just been speaking to Frank. Goodnight, Julian." Senna went into his room and closed the door. Once in his room he rang Galisteu, who had flown to Faro and was now in Senna's house. He sounded "depressed" but said he felt a little better. Galisteu writes (in *My Life With Ayrton*): "The housekeeper interrupted us to try and motivate him by telling him what would be waiting for him on arrival; grilled chicken and steamed vegetables. She handed the phone back to me and we talked about us."

"On race morning," O'Mahony says, "either I would ring him or he would ring me. That morning the phone went (around 7.0) and I knew it could only be him at that time. I picked up the phone and I said 'baggage service!' He'd say something like 'there are four bags to be collected and I'll be at the airport and ready to go at a certain time' – because Ayrton would leave within an hour of the end of the race, an hour and a half." It worked like this: Senna departed for the track, O'Mahony went to the hotel, "beat Valentino figuratively round the ears because he was such a good man and we enjoyed that sort of thing," collected the luggage and proceeded to Forli to await the end of the race and the arrival of Senna. Then he'd fly him to Faro, a journey of "two hours 30 after take off." Estimated time of arrival: the 8.30 which Galisteu counted on.

That morning, Senna checked out of the hotel at around 7.30, simply surrendered the room key at the reception desk. He walked past the wishing well and didn't throw a coin in. He walked through the two electric sliding doors and down some small steps to the carpark and his Renault car. His banker friend Braga went with him. They reached the circuit shortly before 8.0.

That morning a column appeared under Senna's name in a German newspaper, *Welt am Sonntag*. He wrote: "My car reacts a bit nervously to this kind of race surface. This stems from its special aerodynamics but it's also got to do with a difficulty in the suspension." He also wrote: "I pointed out to the directors of the Brazilian and Pacific Grands Prix that we should look more critically at the capabilities of young or inexperienced drivers. My fears were borne out in tragic fashion. I know from my own experience that as a young driver one goes into a race in a totally different way and accepts risks that you shake your head about later."

(It's worth adding an explanation here because what Senna wrote is so important. Newspaper and magazine columns by celebrities may not have actually been written by them. However, in this case the newspaper faxed questions to Assumpcao who secured the answers from Senna – or if the answers were familiar ones which had been used elsewhere, checked with Senna that they were OK – then Jakobi approved the whole. Therefore, the column was authentic Senna.)

When Senna reached the track his face still betrayed profound

BELOW LEFT The small, homely dining room he treasured so much (author).

BELOW Owen O'Mahony, the pilot who flew Senna so far (Owen O'Mahony).

emotions but Frank Williams estimated he'd calmed further. Senna spoke for a while to Niki Lauda about safety then went out in the 9.30 warm-up session where he was decisively quickest (1:22.597 against Hill, next, on 1:23.449).

During it, Senna executed a plot he and Jakobi had hatched on the long haul back from Aida. Prost, who really had been an adversary, would be commentating at Imola for the French television channel TF1, on a programme called *Auto-Moto*. What, Senna mused to Jakobi, if I send him greetings *from the cockpit* as I'm driving round, send him greetings live onto the programme? Jakobi thought that a good idea and, unbeknown to Prost, it was arranged. In the warm-up and above the engine noise Senna suddenly said in English "a special hello to our dear friend Alain. We all miss you Alain." With exquisite forethought, Senna did this on the start-finish straight which, he must have calculated, would be nearer the receivers and thus make for better clarity of reception.

Was Senna tying up more loose ends? There are people who find that conclusion too tempting to ignore; some talk of premonitions. The fact that it had been hatched two weeks before Imola mitigates against such a notion. Nobody, surely, had any premonitions that Imola would be the dreadful weekend, or if they did there are no *facts* to prove they did. We are left with Senna's eminently understandable depression at Imola and no more than the enigmatic and incomplete words of Senna's sister – "he was very low, though I will not say why" – before Imola; left with Senna's own words about the rule changes: "we'll be lucky to get through the season without a major accident."

> When Prost retired and could not threaten, Senna's motivation changed

During this warm-up also (according to Karin Sturm in *Goodbye Champion, Farewell Friend*) Betise Assumpcao claimed, heatedly, to the press that Senna had received a written warning from the Stewards the afternoon before about taking the official car to the scene of Ratzenberger's accident. Since the whole weekend was an accumulation of movements great and small which present a baffling mosaic – and since every detail seems portentous – we had better clear this up. What Assumpcao saw was the written notice to Senna to *appear* before the Stewards, which is what he did. That's not the same thing as a written reprimand which, as Corsmit and Whitaker attest, never happened.

After the warm-up, a strange minuet played itself out between Senna and Prost. Reflecting, Prost says that when he – Prost – retired and could no longer threaten Senna on the track, Senna's motivation changed. "His reasons for living, his reasons for racing in Formula 1 were different." Prost estimates that now the World Championships held a diminished importance for Senna and, although he didn't discuss that often, he did so from time to time with Prost. Equally, Prost estimates that Senna's message on television proved his sincerity.

The warm-up finished at 10.15 and the traditional drivers' briefing would begin at 11. Prost, touched by what Senna had said to him from the cockpit, went to the rear of the Williams pit so that they could talk. Senna was deep in conversation with Brown and Bernard Dudot of Renault, telling Brown not to change anything on the car. From the corner of his eye he noticed Prost and nodded to him, meaning *I know why you've come, I appreciate it and we'll talk when we can.* Prost understood that you don't interrupt a driver when he's deep into a discussion on race morning and, because he understood Senna's behaviour patterns so well, that this discussion might continue for a long time. Prost therefore left. They'd talk another time.

In fact, the discussion ended fairly soon and Senna set off to find Prost; and did find him, but he was deep into a discussion of his own with Louis Schweitzer, President of Renault. Senna would certainly not be so impolite as to intrude, and went to the Williams motorhome.

Towards 11.0 Senna emerged and walked with Berger to the drivers' briefing in the control tower. Whitaker says that "Ayrton arrived with Gerhard from the paddock and you could tell they were talking about something they wanted to achieve during the course of the briefing. I remember Ayrton's mood as very sombre, very sombre. It was well known that there would be a minute's silence at the briefing and there was. Bernie (Ecclestone, President of the Constructors' Association) doesn't play a part in the briefings but he went to the front and announced the minute's silence. They all stood and observed it. Then they started the discussion under the control of Roland Bruynseraede, the race director, who sits there and gives the briefing.

"If you remember, at Aida a 'pace' car had been used on the parade lap (the lap bringing the cars round in grid order for the start) for the first time – because invariably you ended up with the first few drivers waiting for the rear of the grid to arrive and settle. The idea was that the pace car would keep them more bunched. At Aida it was a Porsche 911 and Senna, on pole, felt it wasn't quick enough to allow the Formula 1 cars to heat their tyres properly (speed = friction = heat). You and I might consider a Porsche 911 to be very quick but in comparison with a Formula 1 car it isn't. At Imola they had an Opel turbo which presumably would have created the same problem. Ayrton and Gerhard drew it to the attention of Bruynseraede, it was he to whom this concern was directed. I don't know if the Stewards had already decided not to use the pace car or whether it was Senna's words in the briefing, but it wasn't used." Damon Hill is sure the intervention of Berger and Senna proved decisive.

Tyre temperature is by no means as trivial as it might sound. The Grand Prix car is a very stressed machine, by definition, and exists on fine margins. Cold tyres, when the acceleration bites, can take the car clean off the circuit or make it spin, the last thing anyone wants in the tight-packed scrummage from the grid. Following the same logic, Senna expressed disquiet about the 'safety' car, a saloon which came out in the event of an accident and which the racing cars had to follow until the accident had been cleared up. Then the safety car peeled off, unleashing the racers again but from a rolling start, which meant they'd be up to top speed in a much, much shorter space of time than from stationary on the grid. Senna insisted that the safety car didn't take them round fast enough to *keep* the tyres properly warm.

The briefing over, Senna spoke to Schumacher, Berger and Alboreto about getting all the drivers together on safety. "You'd find," Whitaker says, "that there were many occasions when drivers remained behind to discuss a couple of points. Ayrton was one of those. He was a perfectionist, and if he wanted to discuss something he would discuss it. If somebody else had something for him to do they'd just have to wait." These drivers tentatively agreed to meet about safety on the Friday of the next race, Monaco, which is the only race on the calendar where the usual routine is broken: first qualifying on the Thursday, the Friday being kept free for promotional activities.

The newspaper *Motoring News*, in its issue after Imola, carried this paragraph: "Several drivers reportedly felt the urge to go up to him (Senna) and touch his arm or shoulder at the drivers' briefing, without being able to say quite why." The paragraph was written by David Tremayne, an experienced journalist, and he confirmed to me that some of the drivers had told him this.

Senna went to the Williams motorhome where he and Hill, however reluctantly, gave some Williams guests in the hospitality area their verbal laps of the circuit and chatted as best they could about the weekend. That done, some time past midday, Senna re-entered the motorhome and ate a light lunch. There was a discussion about the race and Frank Williams remembers Senna picking up some spare driving overalls and heading off with them to meet Berger. Williams didn't see him again.

Quite by chance, Prost ate his lunch in the Renault motorhome virtually next to the Williams motorhome – the Williams cars had Renault engines – and, the lunch digested, came out precisely when Senna came out. Prost sensed that this was not the moment: Senna moving into his concentration for the race, wishing absolutely no distractions. The minutes ticking by lock-step to the start.

It was 1.30, 30 minutes to go. Senna saw Prost and waved, again meaning *we'll talk when we can*. Prost noted how astonished bystanders were. Normally Senna and Prost exchanged little niceties when they met and could hardly avoid doing so, but waving affectionately hadn't been seen for years. Prost would remember Senna's look as strange, almost haunted; the pride in his bearing wasn't there. Prost selects these words: "A bit different."

When Senna reached the Williams pit a Brazilian journalist, Jayme Brito, asked him to sign three photographs. Brito has been quoted as saying that "the photos were so sad. I remarked about it." This was even more peculiar than the O'Mahony photographs: not just that they were sad, but in the folklore of Formula 1, less than 30 minutes before a race Senna isolated himself in concentration of other-worldly intensity; would barely recognise a photo of himself, never mind a journalist. He once explained to me that in those moments it is *wrong* to recognise anybody except perhaps your race mechanic. Over the past few years he had become more relaxed, however, and, superficially, this one time, he scanned the photos, signed them and listened to Brito talk about them.

Brito remembers Senna "did something I had never seen him do before. He walked round the car, looked at the tyres and rested on the rear wing, almost as if he was suspicious of the car."

Assumpcao says that *ordinarily* Senna "had a particular way of pulling on his balaclava and helmet, determined and strong as if he was looking forward to the race. That day, you could feel just from the way he was putting on his helmet that he was different. He'd have preferred not to race. He was not thinking he was going to die, he really thought he would win that race, but he just wanted to get it over with and go home. He wasn't there, he was miles away."

At Faro, Adriane Galisteu settled down to watch on television.

At Forli, Owen O'Mahony settled down at the airport to watch on television.

At Sao Paulo, the president of Senna's fan club, Adilson Carvalho de Almeida, and many other members of the 1600-strong club settled down in Senna's business skyscraper to watch on television. They felt close to him in the skyscraper, not a continent and the width of the Atlantic distant.

At Imola, Martin Whitaker settled down in an office adjoining the Media Centre to watch on television. The room, like the Media Centre, was directly above the pits.

At Silverstone, Lyn Patey – an aspiring journalist covering the British Formula 3 meeting there, and a long-time Senna admirer who'd met him in F3 days – sipped coffee in the Marlboro motorhome and settled down to watch on television. She had a very uneasy feeling that "Ratzenberger hadn't been enough of a sacrifice."

At Imola, Assumpcao settled down in the Media Centre to watch on television.

At Newport, in Wales, Mrs Susan Nichols – who had never met Senna but followed his career avidly since 1983, and may be regarded as an atypical supporter – would only watch the warm-up lap.

Once the car had been fired up, Senna completed a lap of the circuit and nosed the car onto his grid position, front and to the left. There, he removed his helmet and balaclava, placing the helmet on the bodywork immediately in front of the cockpit. *Ordinarily* he did not remove his helmet once he'd reached the grid. Each driver prepares in his own way. Some get out of their cars and stand around; some like to wave to the roving television camera which side-steps between the mechanics and the cars; others, like Berger, are just as likely to wander over to the grass beside the track and have a sit-down, a last gorge of mineral water. Invariably Senna remained as near as you can get to motionless inside the cockpit, his daunting eyes locked onto the stretch of circuit ahead. To fiddle around taking the helmet off and putting it back on again could only break the concentration.

Is this trying to fit theory to fact? After all, he'd changed, was more relaxed these days, more likely to do something like that. Whatever, Assumpcao glimpsed Senna's eyes and felt a certain sense of reassurance. Senna, she imagined, was now prepared to do what he did best and do it as well as any man had ever done it. Race.

He summoned a watery smile when the drivers were introduced over the public address and Berger – driving the Ferrari, of course – got a wild cheer. Senna understood about that, the purblind Italian chauvinism, and it seems to have amused him, however many times he had heard it before here, and at Monza for the Italian Grand Prix. He also smiled when Patrick Head, the Williams Technical Director, said something to him. He never, as far as we can ever know, smiled again.

The Ratzenberger aftermath. Professor Watkins explains the situation to Senna while Martin Whitaker (LEFT) waits.

In the pits Frank Williams felt confident. Refuelling stops had been introduced this season, bringing with them a tactical question: how many pit stops a team chose to make. "Ayrton was on a two-stop run, which was going to be quicker than three stops. We did not know Benetton's strategy but Ayrton, we believed, was going to drive away from the others to the point where it didn't matter what they did."

Just before the one minute board was hoisted, Senna put the balaclava on and adjusted it carefully, his strong hands tucking it into the collar of his overalls, smoothing it to his neck. His face seemed morose but that might have been the concentration. It is true he looked miles away, looked to be . . . somewhere else. Maybe he always appeared like that with a minute to go but all these years it had been hidden under the helmet. Maybe not. He put the helmet on and the 25 cars covered the parade lap, felt for their places on the grid in their twin columns.

Susan Nichols felt "what I can only describe as a mounting sense of panic. I said to my husband and daughter 'I can't watch any more because I don't want to see what is going to happen'. It was the first time in over 12 years that I couldn't watch the race. They both thought I'd gone mad. I went into the garden."

When the red light flicked to green Senna made a classic start, onto the power instantly, strongly holding the Williams which wanted to wrestle from him as the power tried to break free. Laying broad, equidistant burn-marks of rubber scrubbed from the tyres by the power, he was already good and clear of the grid and neatly, neatly into the first little left-hander; already decisively ahead of Schumacher.

Behind him, JJ Lehto's Benetton stalled three grid ranks from the one Senna started on. Car after car twisted, darted and missed Lehto. Pedro Lamy (Lotus), unsighted and coming over from the second last rank of the other column, struck the Benetton's rear a mighty blow, so mighty that a wheel was hurled as far as the spectators, causing injury, and the Lotus was hurled across the track. Lehto and Lamy escaped largely unscathed. With debris everywhere, the safety car came out and took the remaining 23 cars round for three laps, overall the 'fourth' of the Grand Prix. On the next lap the safety car signalled – by illuminating the rotating lights on its roof – that it would be pulling off and the race could resume at full bore. Senna's race engineer David Brown radioed what was about to happen and Senna acknowledged it.

The safety car did peel off and again Senna made a classic 'start', onto the power instantly, Schumacher behind, then Berger but already Berger some distance away.

At Silverstone, Patey "sickened by the first incident, waited long enough to see Ayrton safely into the lead after the safety car pulled off and I went to sit outside, unable to shake off a feeling of deep depression."

Now Senna had the powerful, pervading, pounding pressure of Schumacher in pursuit, Schumacher whose Benetton would do 0-60mph in 3.6 seconds, 60-100mph in 1.5 seconds and 100-203mph, its top speed, in 15 seconds; would brake from 203-100mph in 2.3 seconds, 100-60mph in 0.6 of a second, 60-0mph in 1 second. Schumacher could handle all this with complete confidence. Here, already, was a pivotal position in the race which might be pivotal to the whole World Championship.

On that lap six Schumacher thought the Williams looked nervous in Tamburello and was bottoming. Senna led into lap seven, urging the Williams through the hard-right onto the start-finish straight, his hands firm but flexible on the wheel. The white bays of the grid fled beneath the car. He took it over to the right at the little left-hander and kept it on the right along the tree-lined straight towards

Tamburello. The creamy-milky coloured concrete wall in front of the trees seemed to flicker by because of the car's sheer speed. This wall curved round the outside of Tamburello, a looping left which went on and on. Into the mouth of the corner, Senna brought the Williams over towards the red and white painted kerbing on the inside, the classical position for going round.

A camera, and particularly a television camera, distorts distance in width and depth. The television camera which captured Senna assuming this classical position, and whose images would flood round the world, presented Tamburello as a broad, deep place. It is not. It is tight, cramped and narrow. If you stand on the rim of the track and walk directly to the outside wall it is 14 paces.

Senna could see, in panorama.

To his left: the tall, verdant trees, then a wall with mesh fencing above it, then a thin strip of grass, then the red and white kerbing which ended just into the corner.

Directly in front: the width of the track which unfolded out of sight.

To his right: a white boundary line, then a thin strip of grass, then the concrete run-off area, then the low concrete wall with mesh fencing above it, then more trees.

As the loop tightened he placed the car a little further over to the left and passed before a large advertising hoarding for Kronenburg beer. At the point where the red and white kerbing ends, the loop still tightening, he was travelling at 192 miles an hour. The car straightened, which – the loop unfolding left-left-left away from it – took it clean off the circuit and over the thin strip of grass, over the concrete run-off area. It bisected the run-off area and, in the 1.8 seconds before it struck the wall, Senna had clawed the speed down to 131 miles an hour. It was not enough. He sustained devastating head injuries. The distance from the end of the kerbing across the track, grass and concrete to the wall at the angle he went: 102 paces. From 192 miles an hour, and even plough-plough-ploughing the fearsome stopping power of the brakes, 102 paces is a very short distance.

> I didn't need confirmation that Ayrton had been killed. I already knew

It was 2.18 of the hot, dry, sunny afternoon which remains yesterday afternoon.

The Williams bounced from the wall with such force that it reached the rim of the track spinning savagely, thrashed back onto the run-off area and came to rest there. Whitaker watched on the television. "There was an aerial shot and you could see Senna sitting in the cockpit and his head moved slightly. My first thought: *he's had a bad accident but this is his usual way of coming to terms with it*. Normally, if he'd had a big accident or something had happened, he would try and compose himself. Automatically I thought that was what he was doing."

It was the saddest misreading, and one shared.

Adriane Galisteu saw and thought Ayrton would be home to her sooner.

At Forli airport, the man who would have taken him to her, Owen O'Mahony, "simply didn't know Senna's condition" but didn't like the implications of what he was seeing at all.

In Sao Paulo the communal feeling of the fan club found expression in de Almeida. "We were shocked but we were sure we would soon see him walking away from his car with an angry look on his face. He'd been in other accidents that seemed far worse than this one and always walked away."

In Gwent, Susan Nichols "knew instantly what had happened when my daughter told me through her tears that Ayrton had been involved in an horrific accident. I didn't need confirmation that Ayrton had been killed. I already knew."

At Silverstone, Patey sat and "someone gave me the news, almost falling out of the motorhome in his urgency. I leapt to my feet desperate for a TV and more information. As I started to run towards the awning opposite I caught my toe in the bar at the bottom of the Marlboro unit entrance. I fell very heavily on my left side, hitting my head on the concrete and hurting my arm."

In the Media Centre, Assumpcao had seen Senna's head move and went down to the Williams pit where the mechanics were watching on a big screen. She tried to peer between them. Leonardo arrived soon after.

Reportedly, the first marshal to reach Senna, called Stefano Bounaiuto and with 20 years experience, leant towards the cockpit and felt himself recoiling. Afterwards, he wouldn't say publicly what he saw.

Whitaker would, within moments, find himself the only official conduit between the tragedy at Tamburello and the assembled media who would relay it to the world. "If there is an accident, the first thing I do is leave the Media Centre and go straight to the Stewards' Office because, if you like, that becomes the nerve centre. There's a long corridor between the two which is usually so packed with people you can hardly walk along it. I met Alan Henry there (*Guardian* journalist and author) and we were the only people in that corridor. As I saw Alan, I could see he had this look on his face. He looked at me and said 'he's dead'. There was nothing I could reply."

The medical team, Watkins playing a prominent role, tended Senna and removed him from the cockpit, laid him on the ground, continued to tend him. He was alive, but only clinically. The medi-vac helicopter belonging to the Maggiore Hospital, a BK 117, had just dealt with an emergency call at Castel San Pietro – which Senna had left that morning – and was re-routed to Tamburello. It landed on the track five minutes later. Ordinarily this helicopter would be staffed by a doctor and two nurses but now three specialist doctors boarded it to take Senna to the Maggiore. He was lifted carefully inside but it was cramped because the helicopter carried so much life-saving equipment.

At 2.34 it rose above the trees and reached towards its maximum speed of 140 miles an hour. It would take no more than 18 minutes to reach the Maggiore, following the most direct route to Bologna, which was a straight line passing directly over Castel San Pietro. During the flight Senna had a cardiac arrest but the doctors brought him back from that.

O'Mahony knew "as soon as he was put into the helicopter something was seriously wrong." The world did, too.

At Silverstone, Patey had reached a TV in time to see the "feverish activity" before Senna was put into the helicopter but after her fall "a friend took one look at me and despatched me to the Medical Centre where I was inspected and sent on to Northampton General Hospital."

At Imola, Professor Watkins was driven back to the Medical Centre.

Whitaker "told the Stewards I would now be going to the Medical Centre. I had a long-standing agreement with Professor Watkins about how we would cope with such eventualities. At the Medical Centre he would give me a very brief statement on the driver and say if the driver required hospitalisation and which hospital he had

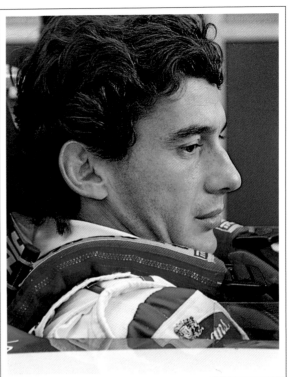

been taken to. I would issue that to the media." By then Assumpcao and Leonardo had arrived there and seen Watkins go in, not seeming to recognise anybody. They asked Whitaker "what's happened? What's happened?" but Whitaker knew no more than they.

Whitaker "asked for Professor Watkins and was shown into a big office. He was sitting there on his own looking at the helmet on the table. I'd seen everything going on, but this was the first time I became aware, the first time I really, really realised something was desperately wrong. Watkins is a professor of medicine, he's seen a lot of things but he was numbed by the whole thing. He looked at the helmet, turned it upside down and walked to the corner of the room and put it down there. He didn't show it to me but I saw the hole in the visor."

Outside, Assumpcao heard someone asking what Senna's blood group was. Jakobi had arrived and suggested it might be in his passport, which was in his briefcase in the Williams motorhome. Assumpcao went there immediately and returned with the briefcase and Senna's mobile phone. No blood group in the passport. Leonardo tried to make a call on the mobile but couldn't get a line.

Inside, Whitaker explained that a statement was necessary, Watkins said Senna had received a "head injury" and Whitaker would draft this into a short, simple press communique. Whitaker asked if he wanted to add anything and Watkins said no, "that's it."

Whitaker left the Medical Centre and Assumpcao asked again "what's happened?" Whitaker was faced with an immediate dilemma. Here was Senna's *brother*. Whitaker suggested they went to the Stewards' Office. "They asked 'shall we come with you?' I said 'it's probably better that I go up the pit lane and you go through the paddock because if we are all seen together people may start drawing conclusions'. We did that." They reached the Stewards' Office and Whitaker asked Leonardo and Assumpcao to wait outside. She realised that she'd left both Senna's briefcase and her handbag at the Medical Centre and hastened to retrieve them. They were exactly where she had set them down.

Inside the Stewards' Office, as Whitaker remembers, "there was complete silence. Bear in mind that at this point I was the only person who had had contact with Professor Watkins. The information he'd given wasn't the sort of thing you'd send over the radio (from the scene). The Stewards were sitting round a table. I said 'I have a statement which I am going to issue but not until I have read it to you so that you know the details of it'. I read the statement – including the phrase *head injury* (author's italics) – and asked if they were in agreement. 'Yes, yes, yes'.

"Bernie was in there. I told him Ayrton's brother and others were outside and suggested somebody should look after him. 'Leave it to me, I'll take them to my motorhome,' Bernie said." (FOCA has a motorhome to rival any other in facilities and privacy.) Whitaker said he would go there after he had issued the statement in the Media Centre. Whitaker read the statement to a "hushed audience" of the media and although more and more questions were fired at him didn't elaborate because he couldn't. He was telling them all he knew.

The helicopter touched down on the Maggiore's helipad, a broad concrete area some 300 metres from the main hospital building with a white painted cross in the middle of it. Ordinarily the staff on the helicopter would transfer their patient to the waiting ambulance but they'd radioed ahead and another specialist team were in the ambulance so that he could be transferred in as little time as possible. As they prepared to transfer him he had a second cardiac arrest but they brought him back from that. Beyond the high fence which separated the helipad from the adjoining road a few people had already gathered and gazed mute. The ambulance reached the Maggiore, a 16-storey L-shaped building, in one minute, reversing up a ramp to the mouth of the intensive care unit.

Under the head of intensive care, Dr. Maria Teresa Fiandri, the staff managed to bring his pulse back to somewhere near normal. "With the first aid at the track, during transport here and in the hospital we did all we could," she said. They put him on a respirator.

At Northampton General Hospital, Patey was "dizzy and in a lot of pain. I was cushioned by the shift in reality facing me. There was a perpetual motion of sick and noisy children, a constant stream of bandaged feet, be-slinged arms like mine, drunk, angry, brawling teenagers and, seemingly ignored by everyone except me, a large TV and video pumping out endless Bugs Bunny cartoons. I suppose I was praying but mainly my mind was blank. I'd had several phone calls from worried friends at the track but only to talk about me and arrange a lift back."

Braga rang his wife Luiza in Sintra, who in turn rang Adriane in Faro, explained how serious Braga told her it was and that they must go to Bologna. Luiza said she'd hire a plane in Lisbon, come to Faro and together they'd fly on to Bologna.

From Forli, O'Mahony began to telephone the hospital "but it was difficult to make them understand I was Ayrton's pilot and not just another fan ringing up." He kept on ringing.

Whitaker went from the Media Centre to the FOCA bus nearby in the paddock. "As I got there Bernie came out to meet me. He said 'what are we going to do now?' Bear in mind we've got camera crews and journalists all around. I said quietly 'first of all we need to get an official statement from the hospital as to what Ayrton's condition is.' He said 'what condition?' He looked at me with that look which says *what are you talking about?*"

Ecclestone: "I thought you said he was dead."

Whitaker (heart sinking): "I didn't say he was dead."

Ecclestone: "You said he was dead."

Whitaker: "No, I said he has an injury to his head."

Ecclestone: "Oh my Good God."

Whitaker realised "this has gone wrong. I thought the 'family' were in the motorhome because Bernie was looking after them. This would have been Bernie's reaction: to take them under his wing. And also Ayrton was an incredibly important part of Bernie's life. They'd been close friends and not many people know that Ayrton had been ski-ing with him and things of this nature" – albeit a long time before.

They agreed that it would be more prudent to enter the motorhome away from the camera crews and journalists. Sanctuary. Everybody, Whitaker remembers, "was in there, including Bernie's wife, and they were numb. People were in tears but I think numbed is the better word. Bernie started to explain that there had been a misunderstanding – Bernie knew the situation didn't look good because he'd heard the original statement I'd read out in the Stewards' Office - but it became apparent that he'd told them Ayrton was dead. Leonardo was sitting in Bernie's chair and was visibly very, very upset. Bernie started to explain and didn't seem to be having a lot of success so I thought that – as the link, if you like, with Professor Watkins – I should try. I said 'in good faith, Bernie has obviously told you something which in actual fact is not quite correct and, although a tragic one, it is a misunderstanding. Here is my notebook and I can show you *Preparing. The grid, Imola* (Colorsport).

and read to you what I did say in the Stewards' room.' I read them the statement."

Assumpcao said: "I don't want to know what you said in the Press Room, I want to know the truth."

Whitaker "looked at her and said 'I've never told you a word of a lie in my life and I'm not about to start right now. Here is my notepad, here is what I wrote down'."

She looked and saw the two words *head injury*.

Whitaker remembers that she said "you're a liar, you're a liar, you're just doing it to cover it up." Assumpcao does not remember saying this but frankly, in the circumstances, it's entirely natural for the participants to find difficulty in retracing exact dialogue. Whitaker left the motorhome, Ecclestone organising for the Senna entourage to go by helicopter to the Maggiore. That also involved organising a car to take them to the helicopter because the track's helipad, on a football field, was some distance away.

The misunderstanding would subsequently assume bitter proportions culminating in the Senna family advising Ecclestone not to attend the funeral in Sao Paulo because he wouldn't be welcome. How did the misunderstanding arise? In the circumstances, every person at Imola on Sunday, 1 May 1994 found themselves in a shifting, cascading nightmare of global consequences and with minimal factual information to go on. Those closest to it felt the weight most. Whitaker is "convinced that although Bernie listened while I read the statement out in the Stewards' room, under the overbearing enormity of the situation, he took the word head for dead. And that was the only word he really heard. I'm sure about that. When I'd said to him that Leonardo and entourage were outside and needed looking after, he assumed it was to comfort them (for a bereavement)." Beyond question Ecclestone acted with propriety and compassion,

> Growing rumours suggested that the facts were being withheld

The race had re-started at 2.55, more or less as the helicopter touched down at the Maggiore. Berger, Senna's great friend among the drivers, led from Schumacher. At 3.15, 20 minutes into the re-started race, Berger lost the lead after nine laps and drifted back. The Ferrari was awkward-handling but Berger had had enough. He retired after 11 laps. His thoughts were on getting to the Maggiore. At the Maggiore, Dr. Fiandri spoke of Senna's "desperate condition."

Whitaker had returned to the Stewards' Office and moved into another nightmare. "The Stewards were there and the director of the circuit and his secretary and a bank of TV monitors and they were watching replays of the incident. We needed the director of the circuit to establish lines of communication with the hospital." What the hospital did have was direct communication with RAI, the Italian television channel, who were broadcasting up-to-the-minute information and inevitably it was looming on some of the screens on the bank of monitors, Whitaker having the words translated. There was a groundswell of rumours suggesting that information was being withheld. Since Whitaker had no official word from the Maggiore, and since in his position he could only relay official words, the nightmare darkened within the wider nightmare.

"We don't have any jurisdiction over a country's medical authorities. To all intents and purposes we are just a racing circuit who want information from a hospital on a racing accident. They don't have to give it to us, and they didn't, they didn't." They did, however, continue to give it to RAI, leading to further confusion. Two laps before the end of the race the following was issued in the Media Centre in an attempt at clarification:

> *As you will be well aware there are numerous rumours circulating*
> *the paddock and here in the Media Centre over the condition of Ayrton*
> *Senna. The organisers of the San Marino Grand Prix are in the hands of the*
> *Maggiore Hospital in Bologna and only the hospital can issue an official*
> *statement on the condition of the driver. Until we receive an official statement*
> *from the hospital there is nothing further we can add. As soon as any official*
> *statement is available we will make sure that you receive it.*

By now TV Globo in Brazil were moving into extreme emotion, with broadcasters struggling to control themselves.

At 4.0 Dr. Fiandri announced Senna as "clinically dead." At 4.05 Father Amedeo Zuffa administered the Last Rites. By now a crowd of some 300 people – who, on the radio or RAI or by word of mouth, had heard where he was – crowded the hospital reception area. It remains staggering that this throng felt a compulsion to go to the hospital. They can't have been active race supporters or they'd surely have been down the road at Imola.

Leonardo, Assumpcao, Lemos and Leberer arrived in the helicopter. Leonardo could have gone in to see Senna but, in the circumstances, decided not to do so.

O'Mahony "eventually got through to the hospital and spoke to Julian Jakobi. Then I flew the plane to Bologna in case Ayrton needed to be taken anywhere." He took off from Forli at 4.15.

At 4.20 the race ended, Schumacher winning it from Nicola Larini (Ferrari) and Mika Hakkinen (Marlboro McLaren). The large crowd, unaware of Senna's true condition, grouped under the podium, waved Ferrari flags and chanted to salute Larini. Then he, Schumacher and Hakkinen attended the mandatory Press Conference. They sat side by side and their faces betrayed that they were lost in another dimension.

At 5.30 at the circuit Martin Whitaker issued a similar verbal statement to the one issued before the end of the race. This again stressed that there were still many rumours circulating about the condition of Ayrton Senna but that no official statement had been forthcoming from the Maggiore Hospital and until this happened there was nothing to add.

At 6.0 Berger arrived at the hospital and was permitted to see Senna. Berger later told Nigel Roebuck of *Autosport* that Senna was still alive when he saw him and "I want that to be known, because various accusations were made at the time, against Bernie Ecclestone, that Ayrton was already dead at the circuit, and Bernie knew about it. That's absolutely not true. I saw Ayrton with my own eyes." Berger flew by helicopter to Bologna airport and "we landed near my plane, which was parked next to his. (In fact where O'Mahony had parked it). Even though I'd just left him, it hit me hard."

At 6.40 Dr. Fiandri announced that "Ayrton Senna died a few seconds ago." The machinery keeping him alive had not been switched off because Italian law forbade it.

The plane which Luiza Braga hired reached Faro and Galisteu boarded it. Galisteu constantly repeated to herself "be strong, be strong" because that is what Senna had taught her to be. The pilot took it to the end of the runway but while he waited for permission to take off for Bologna a message came through. He swivelled the plane and returned to the terminal building. When they deplaned Galisteu started shivering "from head to toe." Luiza Braga received and gave the message and they sat in the terminal for a long time or a short time. Luiza said they'd better go to the house in Faro. There was nothing else they could do. Bologna, a routine hop of maybe three hours, might have been the far side of the moon from them or an infinity further on; and was.

The finality had not been announced at Imola because the fact of it had not been transmitted to Imola. Whitaker, impatience rising around him, hammered at the officials in the Stewards' Office "who were totally embarrassed to even pick up the phone and dial the hospital by this stage." Whitaker found Professor Watkins and between them they fashioned another statement, issued at 7.20.

> *Ayrton Senna suffered severe head injuries which produced a deep coma.*
> *His condition is grave and the electrical brain test shows brain death.*
> *His condition is deteriorating.*

Whitaker qualified it by adding

> *This statement was issued by Professor Watkins from his hotel room in Bologna*
> *some minutes ago. I stress that the information given is his assessment of the*
> *situation before leaving the Maggiore Hospital and travelling back*
> *to his hotel.*

The fax from the Maggiore did not come through to the Stewards' Office until 7.23. It bore the hospital's headed notepaper and, pre-printed, who it was from and how many pages (Pages, 1, including This Page). The typed message:

> *Alle ore 18.40 cessa l'activita cardiaca.*
> *Si constata il decesso.*
> *(At 6.40 the heart stopped.*
> *We verify his death.)*

It was signed-off, in typed block capitals:

> *IL PRIMARIO DEL SERVIZIO RIANIMAZIONE*
> *DOTT. M. TERESA FIANDRI*

but not signed or initialled. Nowhere did it say whose heart had stopped. Ayrton Senna did not need to be named.

All the hospital could do now was set in motion the autopsy, which under law they were obliged to do.

At 7.40 Whitaker read out:

> *The circuit has just received the following official statement from the*
> *Maggiore Hospital in Bologna. 'We verify the death of Ayrton Senna.*
> *The time of death is registered as 18.40'.*

In Sao Paulo, normally a mass of humanity, the streets were emptied. Conjure that image: not a throng but 17 million inhabitants absent from every avenue, every public corner where, of a Sunday, they'd gossip and argue and fall out and fall in again a moment later. The 17 million listened to radios or watched television where, one report says, "newscasters were unable to hide their emotion as they read the tragic news from Italy, but there was also anger in their voices." The presenter who announced the finality said: "All Brazilians feel this as if it were a relative." A few of the 17 million began to drift to the house of Senna's parents in a wealthy suburb. A fraction of the 17 million began to drift to a soccer match where the crowd observed a minute's silence and some of the players sank to their knees for the duration of that, hands clasped in prayer. The silence over, the crowd chanted Senna's name and waved in ripples, waved towards eternity. President Itamar Franco sent his condolences to the Senna family. Senna's Brazilian trainer, Nuno Cobra, broke down during a television interview and murmured "how can this be?"

At Northampton General Hospital, Patey says that about "four hours after I arrived I received my last phone call of the day." A friend in London "had heard of my plight and called to see how I was. I quickly assured her that I would be fine and then asked the question. 'What's happened to him?' There was silence at the other end of the phone, then . . . 'I'm sorry, I thought you knew. We've lost him . . .'"

The toll from the Imola week-end:

Friday – Barrichello's crash at 1.16.

Saturday – Ratzenberger's crash at 1.18.

Sunday – Frenchman Jacques Heuclin injured in a Porsche race before the Grand Prix; Lamy and Lehto crash at the start of the Grand Prix, a tyre injures seven spectators and a policeman; Senna's crash at 2.18; three Ferrari mechanics and a member of the Lotus team injured when a wheel came off Michele Alboreto's Minardi in the pit lane.

O'Mahony made his way to an hotel in Bologna and "we stayed there, Leonardo, Julian and I. Leonardo was the senior family member present, of course, and the Brazilian ambassador came about the arrangements." However routine and necessary these arrangements may have seemed on this Sunday night, they would come to reveal the true scale of what Senna meant. Even those close to Formula 1 were unprepared for the scale: not just Brazil brought to open grief but that rarest of human conjunctions which tran-

The wall
(Colorsport).

scends climates, continents and cultures *and unites*. Self-appointed world statesmen might hope for this but they don't get it.

While the initial arrangements were being made, O'Mahony says, "there was some talk that I was going to have to fly Ayrton back to Brazil." He phoned an engineering company in England who explained that the side-hatch wasn't big enough. "I would have wished to fly him back, oh yes, oh yes. The last part of my contract would have been to deliver him safely home. Put it this way, it would have been a very painful trip, a very painful trip, but it would have been an honour."

On the Monday, mourners were so numerous they provoked traffic jams outside the Istituto Di Medicina Legale, where Senna had been taken at 9.0 the night before and where the autopsy took place. Police ensured the mourners could not enter but a stretcher was brought out so that they could lay flowers upon it. The stretcher quickly overflowed. No statement was made after the autopsy.

At Tamburello flowers were laid.

At the gates of the Williams factory in Didcot, near London, flowers were laid. Richard West, Williams Marketing Director, observed that many of them must have come from people who had never met Senna, never spoken a word to him and maybe never been to a race.

O'Mahony flew the HS125 to Paris, taking Leonardo there so he could board a Varig flight to Sao Paulo. "I parked by the side of the Varig 747. He got out, got into the Varig and I departed. Leonardo was stunned. He did speak a bit but he was stunned. There had been so much responsibility on him, apart from the grief."

O'Mahony flew the HS125 to Southampton, its usual base and where it was serviced. He left it ("it is there to this day") and went home, prepared to fly to the funeral.

On the Tuesday, Senna was flown to Brazil via Paris. An Italian military aircraft had taken him from Bologna to Paris, where he was transferred to a Varig flight. As a mark of respect, the Varig flight cleared a section of their business class for him rather than, as is normal airline practice, find space in the hold.

Meanwhile, the Italian legal system moved. There would be a full investigation and it might be treated as homicide.

In Brazil, Charles Marzanasco, a spokesman for the Senna family, made an appeal on the radio for people not to go to Sao Paulo airport when the Varig flight landed at dawn on Wednesday. There were fears that the city of 17 million would cease to function and if all 17 million went to the airport, grief-stricken and emotionally-charged . . .

"The best way to show your love and respect is to go, in an orderly fashion, to the legislature," Marzanasco said. Senna would lie in state there. Many heeded this. On the Tuesday a column of those wishing to pay their respects began to form outside the legislature. By Wednesday, the column stretched a mile.

Towards dawn on the Wednesday, as the Varig entered Brazilian air space, a flight of jets joined it and fanned out in formation in salute and, unconsciously, to protect the one who no longer needed their protection. As he was brought from the Varig many people wept but some applauded. To applaud a coffin is a poignant act, a last gesture of appreciation but surely also a denial that Senna had died, a denial that he was here but no longer here.

> To applaud a coffin is a poignant act, a last gesture of appreciation

46

An uncounted number of mourners filed by as he lay in state. Almost unnoticed among this throng was Liliane, the woman who had been his wife, who had shared briefly his life and who he had divorced more than a decade before because he'd concluded that his career over-rode his marriage. She made no special arrangements for priority, simply filed by among the throng.

The funeral, after the lying-in-state, made the most profound impression on all who attended it. "I had never seen two million people crying before," O'Mahony says. "You have to remember that Ayrton was all that Brazil had, Ayrton and a soccer team which wasn't doing that well."

Derek Warwick was there, but only after making one of those personal decisions taken behind the barriers. "I'd known Roland Ratzenberger but I could not find a way of getting to his funeral (in Salzburg) the following day if I went to Sao Paulo. I ended up ringing Roland's family and I said 'look, I am very, very sorry. I am not favouring one driver over another, but please understand I raced Ayrton Senna for over a hundred Grands Prix – he had become a friend, an enemy – and I had more respect for that man than any other racing driver I have ever known. I cannot *not* go to Ayrton's funeral'. I almost went to Roland's because I thought that was the right thing to do and, right at the eleventh hour, I said *no, I have to say goodbye to Ayrton*. It was a difficult decision.

"It was very, very special to be a part of the funeral (as a coffin bearer). In myself I felt numb, I felt it wasn't actually happening. It was all a bit of a nightmare. I felt such sadness, and at the same time a kind of happiness to see so many, many people saying farewell to a great driver. Did we fully appreciate the extent of what Ayrton meant to people before that? I'll give you an example. A friend of mine (in Jersey, where Warwick lives) was having some building work done and the day after the accident my friend was showing me round this building. I went into one of the rooms and the workmen were having a tea-break. Each one of them was sniffling. I thought that was strange. None of them were racing people – all football and cricket – but they'd just been reading about the accident."

In fact, quite unknown to Warwick, it would have been possible to attend both funerals because Johnny Herbert and Berger managed that. Berger felt an eerie sense that Senna was watching the extraordinary vastness of the funeral, on a presidential scale but with the emotion on top, and that Senna the perfectionist would have been annoyed if anyone had put a single step out of place.

Herbert was "a bit disappointed" that more drivers did not go because "there was only really a handful of us who went to either. I know it affects different people in different ways and I understand that but to me it was a matter of showing respect. I knew Senna well enough to joke around with him and have little chats with him. He'd joke around with me. I got on well with him. I'd known him a little bit in karting, I'd raced with him twice there – once in Italy and once in Sweden: 1982, he'd reached Formula Ford 2000 but he was so desperate to win the World Championships he competed in that one event."

Winners are often desperate to win, but none more so than Ayrton Senna.

Once upon a time, many years before the circuit of Imola was built, the parkland in which it stands was a favoured walking place on a Sunday. In those days people gathered in a quiet corner by a fountain and listened to a little band which played a special kind of drum, a tamburello. Its sound has long gone from there. On Sunday, 1 May 1994, in the looping corner which bears the name of the drum and close to the old fountain, it was replaced by a sound from hell.

CHAPTER THREE

A time
to plant

As explained in the Introduction, in recreating aspects of Ayrton Senna's life and career up to Tamburello I went looking behind the milestones. What follows is not an exhaustive compilation, not a slog through it all again but, I hope, something else entirely.

A conundrum, right at the beginning. Given the kart at four, Senna couldn't drive competitively until he was 13, in July 1973, but evidently he did. His sister Lalli says that, as a child, Senna was always picking fights with bigger boys which, in a sense, he'd continue to do for the rest of his life. She adds that "his eyes had real sweetness in them, you know. Everyone said so." His mother Neide says that he was clumsy as a small lad, would fall going up stairs and she'd always buy him two ice-creams because he'd drop the first. Learning to control the kart taught him co-ordination, perhaps even delicacy, of movement.

The kart assumed more and more importance, Senna took it seriously and father Milton realised he would have to take it seriously too. Senna once said that he first competed at the age of eight, which is the conundrum since he ought to have waited another five years. Senna, however, didn't make mistakes about matters like his races and it must have been so. He'd remember the grid was decided by drawing lots and he drew Number One. He'd also remember older, bigger boys were in it but "I was small and light so my kart was fastest on the straights with the weight advantage I had." The big boys might draw up in the corners but *Senninha* bombed along those straights. Another kart touched him with three laps to go and he went off.

At 13, a week before Senna's 'official' debut at Interlagos, Milton invited a man called Lucio Pascual Gascon – known as Tche – to his office in Sao Paulo. Tche, a Spaniard who had been a military engineer and emigrated to Brazil some quarter of a century earlier, was a famed kart engine tuner. He'd worked with Emerson Fittipaldi and Carlos Pace. Fittipaldi reached Formula 1 in 1970, Pace in 1972. Of his karting days, Fittipaldi writes "they are better than motor cycles, because they are on four wheels and give you a better idea of what it is like in a big racing car. They give you the same knowledge of sliding, of taking the right line – and in go-karts there is a lot of competition. You can learn how to overtake on braking, how to 'close the door', and all this does not cost a lot of money. It doesn't look it, but go-kart racing is very quick, the acceleration is incredible."

In July 1973 Tche already knew a bit about Senna because he'd seen him practising at Interlagos and felt he had a future. The Spaniard would now work for Senna preparing the kart. As we approach the race, it's tempting to envisage that Senna, just into his teens, was already the person the world would come to know, the traits already firmly in place and non-negotiable all the way to Tamburello, 1 May 1994. Tempting? Oh yes. He won . . .

In January 1976, he and Milton travelled 45 minutes from their home to Interlagos to watch a qualifying session for the Brazilian Grand Prix, opening round of the Grand Prix season. Here Senna saw the great ones of the day, Fittipaldi and Pace, Lauda, James Hunt, Jochen Mass, John Watson, Jody Scheckter, Jacques Laffite, Carlos Reutemann and, in the beautiful black and gold Lotuses, Ronnie Peterson and Mario Andretti. Evidently young Senna sat on a wall watching entranced. He cannot surely have known he was watching his own future.

Eight years hence, the 'new' Nurburgring was opened in Germany with a race of identical Mercedes saloons. Among others, Lauda, Reutemann, Watson, Scheckter, Hunt and Laffite took part. Guess who *won*? Nine years hence Senna put a beautiful black and gold Lotus onto pole in Portugal, first of his Formula 1 career. The race was run under streaming, standing-water conditions and seven cars spun helplessly off. Guess who won?

In karting, Senna took the Sao Paulo Championship in 1976 and finished third in the Brazilian Championships. The year after, he took the South American Championships in Uruguay. Tche has said that Senna "always came to a race to win it. For him, the others didn't exist." Tche would tell him to "keep cool, keep cool" but Senna would reply "no, for me it's first place or nothing." Tche judges the young Senna "an individualist, always seeking perfection."

> He proved to himself that the world held nothing to fear and that he could conquer it

It was time to look further afield to broaden the career, deepen it, move it forward. Further afield was Europe, where he'd never been before. By a happy coincidence, the Brazilian Karting Federation were keen for some of their better young drivers to sample the World Championships at Le Mans, France, in September 1978. No Brazilian had contested these Championships since 1974. What happened at Le Mans – and what happened the following year at Estoril, Portugal – is described in some detail (seemingly trivial incidents included) using the contemporary source of *Karting* magazine's reportage as well as original interviews, because the two competitions reveal far more than, as the saying goes, that the child is the father of the man. At 18 Ayrton Senna came to an unfamiliar continent and handled that. He came among strangers from many places who all wanted to beat him (and each other) and he handled that. He measured himself against the best on the planet and he handled that. In 1978 and 1979 he proved to himself that the world held nothing to fear and he could conquer it. From this, all else flowed.

"I had never heard of Ayrton Senna before," Angelo Parilla says. "A friend of my father had a big company in Sao Paulo producing tables and chairs. He had two sons racing in karting and he was friendly with this Ayrton Senna, who was also racing. Ayrton wanted to compete in the World Championships so he got in touch with this man and this man got in touch with me and asked, was it possible for me to help this young guy?" The Parilla family made karts in Milan: a small but effective firm who manufactured all components except the tyres. The karts were called

This is the range of emotions Senna could summon at a Press Conference. They were taken in Adelaide, 1989.

The fastest men on earth. Senna with sprinter Carl Lewis in Japan (John Townsend).

DAP. "I said it was possible and asked for something like $6000, $7000 for the equipment, mechanics, everything.

"Before he came to Milan his father rang me up and said Ayrton only liked Brazilian food and even when he was in other South American countries he wouldn't eat until he got home! I thought we'd see about that. The boy took the plane and I met him at Milan airport. I didn't know what he looked like but I did know he had two sponsors, Coca-Cola and a Brazilian company, Gledson. He wore a Gledson hat so I recognised him. He didn't speak much Italian and I spoke 10% Portuguese. It was 11.0 in the morning and I decided we'd go to a good Italian restaurant to see what the boy did like to eat. It was a Florence-style restaurant where they have good meat. (You have to imagine that what follows must have been enacted with gesturing, pointing and a verbal struggle for mutual comprehension.)

Parilla: "What would you like?"

Senna didn't know, of course.

Parilla: "Do you like spaghetti?"

Senna: "I've never eaten spaghetti before but I'll try it."

Parilla ordered spaghetti carbonara (coated with minced ham and a creamy sauce) and the boy wolfed it.

Parilla: "Do you want wine?"

Senna: "No, water, thanks."

Second course Parilla ordered pork and the boy wolfed that, third course dessert, wolfed that.

Parilla: "Coffee or cognac?"

Senna: "No, I don't drink coffee or cognac. Water, thanks."

Parilla: "Is there anything else you want?"

Senna: "Spaghetti carbonara again, thanks."

Parilla: "Yes, OK, but you can't have the whole meal again, it's beyond my pocket!"

Thus a friendship was born; and it endured. (When Senna returned to Brazil, evidently he said Brazilian food was terrible . . .) The first few days, Senna staying in a modest local hotel, were awkward. In fact "it took a few days because he spoke very few words of English, probably 50 words, and we tried it in English and that was a disaster. So we evolved something which was between Portuguese, Spanish and Italian and we found out that that worked. His family was very, very rich and at home he lived like a king. Here in Italy he was staying in a small hotel, could hardly speak a word of the language so the first 10 days were really hard for the boy. Those 10 days were important because he was proving to himself that he didn't have to stay in Brazil for the rest of his life. And whenever he drove the kart, immediately everything else vanished for him.

"He was a strange young man, a nice boy, he looked in good condition, didn't give any trouble at all, very quiet, but he seemed strange because he was an 18-year-old who was only interested in going to the track with the kart and testing it. Nothing else. He wasn't interested in going into Milan to have a look at the shops, even" – never mind the other delights of Italy, many of them dusky and female.

In August, Senna tried the DAP at Parma, a track more than 100 kilometres from Milan and what Angelo Parilla described as "difficult." It's a continuous snake-like unfolding of corners. Terry Fullerton, also a DAP driver and World Champion in 1973, was there and it went like this: for almost a week Fullerton tested and evaluated between *Angelo Parilla holding a favourite photograph of Senna* (author).

30 and 40 engines and then Senna ran them. Towards the end of the week, Angelo's brother Achille said to Senna *OK, go for it*. Angelo records that "Senna did 10 laps and he did the same time as Terry. This was astonishing. Parma is difficult, and he'd not driven before on Bridgestone tyres. He'd been used to Brazilian tyres at home. To drive on Bridgestone soft tyres was not easy, so what he did was astonishing."

In the small karting community word soon spread. A Yorkshireman and driver, Mike Wilson, says "there'd always been fairly good Brazilians but nobody exceptionally good. First thing I heard was that Fullerton had been doing some lap record times at Parma with a Brazilian sat about two inches off his back bumper bar keeping up with him. In fact, that was the first thing I'd ever head about Senna. I hadn't actually seen it."

Parilla remembers that "a week after Ayrton arrived, Tche flew to Italy. He didn't work on the kart, he just came to support Ayrton like a father-figure. The combination between Tche and Ayrton was very, very close. Tche came at his own expense, and he's not a rich man. Ayrton was lucky that Tche came because he could speak Portuguese to him, and that made him feel more at home."

The little Parilla team (six or seven plus drivers) set off for Le Mans in a car and two vans and when they reached the town in France, famous for its 24-hour sports-car race, they booked into the Ibis hotel. Le Mans was manifestly not Italy in its architecture, language or food. Senna would have to handle the transition. He did.

And the stranger came to Le Mans, which *Karting* described as "a purpose-built track of the traditional Continental sinuous type." The stranger came to compete with the drivers who'd been around, Fullerton, an American called Lake Speed, and Wilson, to select just three. The Brazilians apart, entries were from Austria, Belgium, Switzerland, France, Germany, Denmark, Britain, Italy, Norway, Holland, Sweden and the USA.

(To avoid confusion, please remember that Senna's full name was Ayrton Senna da Silva and he didn't shorten it to Senna for a couple of years, and only did shorten it because Senna was, he felt, more distinctive. Da Silva is a common name in Brazil.)

Karting wrote "the second heat contained the new European individual champion Pierre Knops of Belgium and the extremely rapid Senna da Silva of Brazil using DAP equipment. He was only in this series of heats because of a substantial penalty after a high noise reading in the time trials. It was a nice clean start and the Brazilian rapidly disappeared into the distance never to be challenged." The reporter added naughtily that "just like the scene at the guillotine during the French Revolution, the French nurses knitted patiently at the first corner, watching the accidents appreciatively."

Senna won the third heat, but in the sixth "an early lead was lost when he had to retire." In describing the Time Trials section after the heats, *Karting* pointed out that "the Brazilian Senna da Silva arrived in Europe just 10 days previous to the Championships. By putting up third fastest time with his compatriot (Mario S. de) Carvalho fifth, Brazil was suddenly a force to be reckoned with and there was the intriguing possibility of the Championship going to a non-European for the first time."

This second section of Time Trials comprised six heats. "Initially (G) Leret had the lead from Senna da Silva in the second heat but the Frenchman appeared too inexperienced at this level of competition and was squeezed out by the Brazilian. There then occurred

RIGHT Senna's kart (plus sponsor's sticker) still stands in the foyer of the Parilla factory in Milan (author).

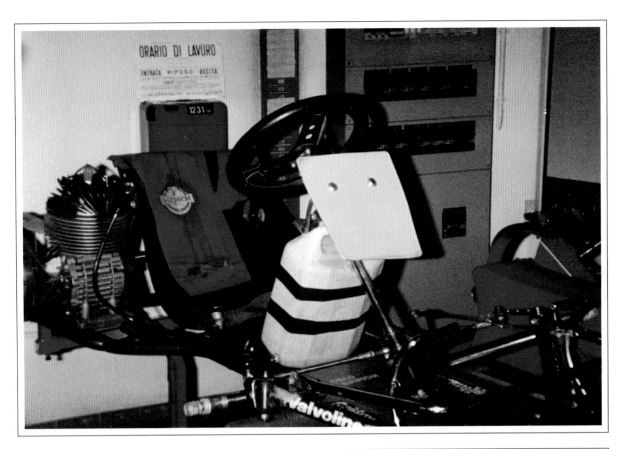

LEFT Silverstone, 1992. The Allsport caption reads "Ayrton Senna looks to the Heavens for more power" (Allsport).

yet another of those strange coincidences that seemed to dog the whole event, and which, although not significant individually, perhaps are worthy of note when viewed in retrospect. We had the flying Brazilian out front followed by (Toni) Zoeserl and Leret. The leader started to slow so that the gap very rapidly diminished to zero then Senna da Silva parked on the grass. The race director prepared to black flag Zoeserl for knocking off the leader. What is of interest here is that this action was the first and only time the race director seemed interested in taking action for alleged bumping tactics and it would have resulted in a Frenchman winning the race. Fortunately he was persuaded to go to the Brazilian's kart and see for himself that the retirement was because it had seized and not because of being hit. It was a close call and many felt jittery at the thought that the Championship might be at the mercy of impetuous officialdom."

In the last heat, Corrado Fabi's early lead was "destroyed by Senna da Silva who dragged (Georg) Bellof with him after the latter had only just made the start following a rapid kart change on the rolling lap. They scrapped around with Fabi taking second place only for him to spin while trying to get back in front."

The finale comprised three runs. In the First Final Senna finished seventh. In the Second, "Senna da Silva was really steaming and effortlessly dispatched Leret." Later, "Speed led Senna da Silva, Mickey Allen and (Lars) Forsman with all knowing that if the American could hang on to the lead until the end he would be Champion. At one stage the Brazilian drew alongside Speed and gained about three inches only for Speed to coolly shut the door at the next corner."

These many years later, in a drawl straight from his native Jackson, Mississippi, Lake Speed remembers this.

"I took up karting because it was one of those deals where a kid down the street got a go-kart and every child in the neighbourhood had to have one. That was fun karting. It started to get serious when I was about 13. It was also kinda funny because I only came over to Europe once a year for the World Championships, whereas the others had been racing each other all season long. No, no, I hadn't heard of Senna before Le Mans, I didn't know a thing about him.

"Everyone there was talking about this guy who was a hot runner from Brazil, and he was a factory driver for DAP which meant he was one of their front-runners. You've got to keep your eye on the competition a little bit but, no, I really didn't know him. Me just coming in for the World Championships, I was pretty much an outsider. We were at the far end of the pits, about as far away from everybody else as you can get. We didn't even have a stand to put the kart on, we were using a big trash barrow.

"I had one close encounter with him on the track. I was leading the race and Senna had worked his way up to second. I could *feel* someone behind me, one of those instinct things. Sometimes you just know, or maybe it's the sound that you hear. Past the pit area there was a 180-degree right turn and I just *felt* he's gonna try and beat me there, he's gonna try and outbrake me. I was going as hard as I could go.

"I stayed to the left and mentally I paused, I reasoned, and yes, he was trying to outbrake me, yes, he was comin' by but he was going too *hot* and he went off. If

> Everyone was talking about this guy who was a hot runner from Brazil

A decade after Parilla, Senna still eats spaghetti!

I'd turned in we'd have had a crash. I never saw him again in the race. You understand, with an incident like that, well, the competition is so close anyway and at Le Mans it really, really was close.

It gets to people. It got to him and he went for it and I recognised he was going to go for it. If I'd tried to fight him it would have cost me or both of us, but as it was I let him go and he was going too hot."

When Speed says "going off" he doesn't mean a tremendous crash because Senna recovered quickly, but . . . not for long. *Karting* says he was "using broad new tyres for each race with the 7.0 size on the rear whilst Mickey Allen was having to use the 6.5s as he didn't have the latest style to match the wide rears. Perhaps this was the reason for the ensuing tangle or perhaps it was a tactical error, but as Mickey challenged the Brazilian so he appeared to be unable to match the adhesion of the other and the resultant collision put them on the grass, with only Allen restarting."

In the Third Final, now irrelevant because Speed had the title, "Mueller, Allen and Senna da Silva were having a mighty fight which resulted in more than one collision." Speed finished in fourth place, de Bruyn fifth, Senna sixth, Wilson eighteenth.

What really happened at Le Mans? "There were superior compound tyres supplied by Bridgestone," Parilla says, "and we tried to get a set for Ayrton but Bridgestone refused. They said it was too late, it wasn't possible, this and that, so I bought a set – they weren't the best, they were medium good I would say – from another Italian team, Bira. We paid 800,000 lira (around £400). We saved the special for the Finals and before them, in the second heat, Ayrton ran standard compounds and was leading immediately. He went away from everybody, went away at probably 10 metres a lap, which was astonishing to see. He was unlucky because the engine blew up.

"In the First Final he started sixteenth on the grid and finished seventh. When he came in he said 'I need a different sprocket, then I can go a lot quicker.' We changed it and in the Second Final he was (almost) leading then he had the accident with Allen. In the Third Final he had to run on standard compounds because by then the specials were really destroyed. He was disappointed because he could have won the World Championship. My personal opinion is that the first year he came to Europe he was absolutely unbeatable (if he had the right tyres, the engine didn't blow and he didn't crash). He knew nothing about Europe, he knew nothing about the European drivers but he was in absolutely 100% perfect condition. *And after Le Mans he realised he was good enough to win.*"

During Le Mans, Speed spoke not one word to Senna. Nothing sinister, Senna was only another competitor, one of the many.

During Le Mans, Peter de Bruyn spoke not one word to Senna. "We were in different teams, of course, he was racing for DAP, me independent. I always stayed by myself, I never drove for an official factory. In karting we were all a little bit close in that maybe drivers would talk, maybe not, but you certainly wouldn't spend all day together."

During Le Mans, Mike Wilson spoke not one word to Senna. Nothing sinister, Senna was only another competitor who'd been sixth in the Championship, might never be seen again, might never return. *Another Brazilian who came and went, and what was his name again?* Senna was learning of the distances you keep between yourself and the others, learning that they all badly want to win and you have to want it more than them. From this, also, all else flowed.

He'd return, all right, and they'd start speaking to him and he to them, and – in 1989 and 1993 – he'd show Wilson such kindness

The shoot-out at Thruxton for the Formula 3 championship. Senna leads while Davy Jones (car No 1) and Martin Brundle lock wheels rather than horns (John Townsend).

that even today the Yorkshireman can't bring himself to watch a Senna video, of which he has several, to the end. (Incidentally, of the complete entry in 1978, only Senna would reach Formula 1.)

After Le Mans the Parilla team returned to Italy and flew to Sugo, Japan, for a race there. "In Sugo he was really quick," Parilla says. "In Timed Qualification he came fourth but as usual with him he had a big problem with the front tyres. They were good for three or four laps and then he destroyed them because that was his style of driving. In the Final he ran second, had more problems with tyres and finished fourth. We knew he'd return to Europe the following year because he wanted to win the World Championship. It was the biggest thing he wanted. In fact, he flew from Japan to Brazil and we flew back to Italy and we brought his driving overalls, to keep for him for the following year.

RIGHT Tasting McLaren's Formula 1 power, 1983, under the watchful eye of Ron Dennis (John Townsend).

BELOW RIGHT Tasting Brabham's Formula 1 power, 1983, under the watchful eye of designer Gordon Murray

"And the following year, a week or two before he was due to arrive, we took the overalls to have them cleaned so he'd look proper. When he arrived and saw them he started to cry. He didn't expect people to care about him like that. He was a nice guy, a really nice guy who became a sort of son to us. He stayed with us, not in an hotel. My house was small, my brother's house was small, so he stayed one week with me, one week with my brother and we sent him for one week to our mother!

"He arrived in May and was with us five months, more or less. He never contacted home and nobody from home called him. I don't know if it was deliberate, I don't know if he was proving his manhood. A few times, a very few times, I tried to ask him about his mother, about his father, but there was no reply really. It's a strange story. It was also something which astonished me. I'd say 'look, you want to call, you can call' but no he didn't want to. It's normal to call home now and again. Was it part of becoming a man? I just don't know. Strange, really strange."

In 1979 Senna raced in the Champions' Cup at Jesolo in May – and at San Marino, Wholen in Switzerland and Parma – as well as the World Championships. Jesolo has nestled into karting folklore. "In practice," Parilla says, "he did a lap, two laps, he came in and said 'one front tyre is bigger than the other.' I said 'no, no, impossible.' He said 'yes, one tyre is bigger than the other.' We checked and he was right: one tyre *was* bigger – by a *millimetre*. Also in practice he had a big crash. My wife took him to hospital, they checked him over and nothing was broken. He came back and raced. We put him in the driving seat because it wasn't possible he could put himself in it. He held position two or three in the race – but after the crash we'd moved the engine from one frame to another, and that had to be done quickly because there was no time. The mechanics did not discover that the carburettor had been damaged on the bottom and he broke down."

Senna was becoming noticed. At Jesolo, a journalist asked him about the extent of his future. "A kart driver to reach Formula 1?" Senna mused. "For the moment I do not think about it. Brazil already has Nelson Piquet (in his first full season with Brabham, a leading Formula 1 team) and is keeping precious the heritage of Emerson Fittipaldi (World Champion in 1972 and 1974 and still driving for the Copersucar team)."

"It was good to race against Senna, really good," de Bruyn says. "I found him very hard with himself. I saw races where something happened to him, he went off the circuit, was taken to hospital, came back, raced again. I remember at Jesolo the

Two portraits of Senna, 1984 (LEFT Nigel Snowdon *and* RIGHT Sporting Pictures UK).

mechanics had to lift him into the kart to race. It was difficult to believe what he demanded of himself. I think, that time at Jesolo, he crashed four times. I understand he was hard on the team, hard on the mechanics but hard on himself, yes, but that is the way I see a racing driver must be. If you want to succeed, and also succeed in everyday life, you must accept that you have to give 100%, and that is what he was giving."

Mike Wilson did "start speaking to him in 1979. We'd had a bit of an accident together at Jesolo. It was one of the rounds of the European Championship and the way my kart had been set up I had a few problems, my kart was slidey. Once I got better grip from the tyres my lap times got better and better, whereas Senna was really quick for the first five or six laps in every heat. He was behind me so, down the straight, I held the inside line to try and keep him behind – I wasn't zig-zagging – knowing that if he did get past it would be difficult for me to repass him.

"He pushed me a couple of times to try and get me out of his way, just touched the back bumper bar to knock me wide, but I managed to keep the kart on the inside. Then on I think the third lap and at the end of the straight – where there was a fast right-hand corner to a hairpin – he lunged down the inside as I was turning in to the corner. All of a sudden, he was there and it was absolutely impossible to avoid touching each other. Unfortunately we did touch and he turned over and ploughed into the fence. He went completely over two or three times.

"He'd already had a bad accident in practice. At that time the tyres we were using were very, very sticky and it was easy to lift the kart on to two wheels. On the Friday – the race was on a Saturday – he went onto two wheels on the fastest corner of the

RIGHT *The Toleman at Monaco, 1984, qualifying.*

The Toleman racing to second place, Monaco, 1984 (John Townsend).

circuit and that also sent him into the fence. So he was injured before he even started the race.

"After it, we had an argument at the circuit and then we also had a bit of an argument in the evening at the prize giving. It was in the centre of Jesolo and, if memory serves me, I'd been third. When we had the accident I suffered a puncture which didn't help, you know. I went up for a trophy and, as I was coming back with it, I walked in front of him, not particularly knowing that he was sat there. He turned around and said 'you stupid idiot' or something like that. I replied 'eff off,' that sort of thing, as people unfortunately do. From that accident we were never really friends." Not yet. It makes the kindness in 1989 and 1993 all the more remarkable.

The race at San Marino, Parilla explains, "really was at San Marino: a street race, a difficult and dangerous circuit. Ayrton was leading the Final, like usual, by a long way (and lapping slower karts). There was a big accident at the chicane, karts everywhere, ambulances. It looked like there was only one path through the wreckage and Ayrton went into it but he couldn't get through and stopped so the whole circuit was blocked. The organisers decided that was the end of the race and he'd won!"

The 1979 World Championships were at Estoril, where Senna (whom *Karting* now named as Ayrton Silva) finished second overall to a Dutchman, Peter Koene. Here Senna competed against someone he'd meet in Formula 1, Aguri Suzuki. De Bruyn did start to speak to him, the distances diminishing, but "when I did I saw him as a strong competitor. A very strong one (chuckle). He was very, very fast at times but he didn't use the brakes properly. That was a lack of experience, because he made quite a lot of tactical mistakes. In racing he was a hard man, to talk to he was polite and nice, very polite actually."

The karting rules had changed. In the finale, a driver's two best finishes counted from the three Finals with the grid positions for the First Final being used if a tie-break were needed. (Parilla describes this as "crazy, crazy, absolutely crazy.") That grid, pole to the right:

De Bruyn (NL)

Wilson (GB)

Schurman (NL)

Yasutoshi (J)

Giugni (I)

Koene (NL)

Senna (BR)

Nielsen (DK)

In the First Final, *Karting* reported that "to a roar from the crowd, Silva passed Koene into the lead. Silva enjoyed seven laps of lead until de Bruyn tigered back. Suddenly this intense pace and close competition – in effect we had a solid 20 kart long queue – resulted in Silva slipping back so the three Dutchmen (de Bruyn, Koene and Harm Schurman) held the first three places in the Championship!" De Bruyn won, Koene second, Senna fifth.

The Second Final. De Bruyn had pole and a win would give him the Championship, as Senna well knew. "Not surprisingly de Bruyn was in the lead as they snaked through the first right-then-left bend closely followed by Koene, Schurman, Sugaya Yasutoshi and Silva," *Karting* reported. "In characteristic flamboyant style, the Brazilian took them one by one until he was behind the leader – the master blocker. De Bruyn's hand shot up indicating he had a problem: a broken chain. For the last

The Toleman, too close for comfort (John Townsend).

six laps it was the DAP team with the nervous twitch, because Koene was pressing Silva hard and both were driving DAPs. One incident could so easily have eliminated both. With three laps left, Koene got past Silva without an entanglement." Koene won, Senna second.

The organisers deliberated for an hour and a half to be sure they understood the permutations. If de Bruyn won the Third Final he'd be Champion. If Koene won he'd be Champion. If Senna won he'd have a first place and a second, but so did Koene – and Koene had it on the dreaded grid place tie-break from the first leg.

Ayrton, you're not World Champion, you're in position second

Karting reported that "the track surface temperature had dropped 10 degrees Farenheit. No team orders were given, just Peter and Ayrton walking quietly together to discuss that – because, as there was no way the latter would be Champion, there was no objection to him winning the Third Final. All that mattered was that they shouldn't wipe each other out in a brief moment of glory to let de Bruyn through." There is extreme doubt about this. The evidence points to the fact that Senna *did not know*.

Because the organisers had deliberated for the hour and a half "it was almost dark. The enormous stands were packed with fans jeering and whistling at the delay, with a former British team manager proud of his part in winding-up the spectators with cat-calls and stamping," *Karting* reported. "De Bruyn led but a mechanical problem halted him. A yellow DAP sweater, waved at Koene, was the signal that he could relax if he wished." Koene had already given Senna an "easy opportunity" to go past. "The spectators knew the drivers' nationalities, if not the subtleties of the points scoring system, so when Silva took over the lead there was a tremendous roar of appreciation for the Brazilian (the umbilical cord between Portugal and Brazil). Responding to the encouragement of the public and mechanics waving anything that bore the DAP name, Silva adopted a dashing driving style, with rapid flicks and swoops, in the twilight." Senna won, Koene sixth to give, overall, Koene and Senna on two points but no escaping the tiebreak. If the rules had not been changed, Senna would have been World Champion, the only title in his career which he contested and did not win. Specifically:

	Koene	Senna
First Final	2	5
Second Final	1	2
Third Final	6	1

"He lost just by the rules," de Bruyn says. I say to de Bruyn that this irritated Senna (or worse) long after. "You say he was still upset about it 10 years later well, yes, that must be. At Estoril, the two drivers who should have won it (de Bruyn and Senna) did not win it! You have a depth of feeling. All the good drivers have that. There's nobody who goes home laughing if they've lost. When I lost in 1979 I did not race again for three months. I was completely fed up with everything. Your whole career is to beat the best, to win the World Championship. You can be five times second but it's better to be one time first, no? So when something like that happens, when you think you're going to win and you don't, it's difficult to express what feelings you get. I still have the same now (1995). I run a lot of drivers in karts and every time we lose I feel sick. I think it's normal."

In a magazine called *Kart and Superkart*, a journalist wrote: "Da Silva crossed the line the jubilant winner of the last Final, thinking he had won the World title. The scenes were something else. Everyone, including me, was wandering round thinking da Silva was World Champion and indeed da Silva was ecstatic with joy in his pit, but down the other end of the pits Koene was being hugged and kissed by all and sundry, obviously realising *he* had made it. The scene changed dramatically a few moments later when da Silva had had the situation explained to him, and was inconsolably sobbing in the back of the DAP pits, where a DAP mechanic was also in tears – either of joy at a DAP win or of sorrow at da Silva's misfortunes! Between the two stood Angelo Parilla, not knowing whether to laugh or cry in his greatest moment of triumph."

Brian Hart, who made the Toleman's engines. "In this picture," Hart says, "I'm clearly telling Senna something. In those days it was about 50–50, us telling him and him telling us" (John Townsend).

Parilla remembers that in the "First Final, Ayrton felt something wrong, he was checking the engine all the time and he was fifth. My brother checked the engine and found the problem. Ayrton started sixth in the Second Final and finished one metre behind Koene. He started the Third Final like a rocket and (at one stage) he was going away at 20 metres a lap. At Estoril they used the grandstand which they use for the Formula 1 Grands Prix and it was full, 10,000, 20,000 people. You have to realise this was Portugal, you have to realise the links with Brazil, all the crowd were for Senna. He was going along the straight in front of the grandstand punching the air. My brother and I knew he wasn't Champion but he didn't know. He finished the race, he was jumping around, he was kissing everybody. Between my brother and I, we said we have to tell him. I said 'look, Ayrton, you're not World Champion, you're in position second.'

*Senna slides off at
Turn One, Detroit, and
is theatrically helped
away* (John
Townsend).

The boy cried like I've never seen anybody cry in my life.

"I still say he wasn't second at Estoril but he *won*. Normally, if people have the same number of points, who wins the Last Final is Champion and it had been like this for ever and ever. They changed that and it was decided by a grid position – crazy, crazy, absolutely crazy."

To all intents and purposes, Senna remained another karter, albeit a fast and determined example of the species. He wasn't. Perhaps the first authentic piece of Senna mythology lies here. Reflecting, de Bruyn says "for me the most interesting thing with Senna in karting was that – maybe because I had problems in finding grip – he always had a lot of it. He was constantly going onto two wheels and having to control the kart like that because of too much grip, but he could control the kart on two wheels. The control was not the problem for him but it was for most of them, they could not do it (chuckle). In those days, if you had big grip you slid a lot. I tried to find grip by using the settings on the kart, but he gained a great deal of it by pushing very hard. He was one of the first to run wide settings on the rear, for example. I was running narrow for grip and he already had too much! That showed he had a certain style, a certain way of driving. This grip must have come from the way he drove because the others did not have it. I don't know how to explain it, I just don't know. Probably it was the way he pushed the kart into the corner – he told me later that he never understood how it was possible we were running *our* settings! He did not understand how I could drive with the narrow. He'd thought about those things, like he always did."

BELOW Attention to detail with the model aeroplane.

BELOW RIGHT A little fine tuning, Silverstone, 1988 (Nigel Snowdon).

De Bruyn is reiterating the accepted wisdom: wider = less, narrower = more. "I presume he was at least five, six centimetres

wider in the rear. He could only handle that because of the way he drove and it was fascinating to watch."

The astonishing victory in the wet at Estoril, 1985. Here he is overtaking Eddie Cheever's Alfa Romeo.

Mike Wilson explores the mythology. "What Peter de Bruyn says is correct, but I don't think Peter knew that Senna used a wheel-base which was 101cms and the karts we were using were 104: the shorter the wheel-base the more grip the kart would give you. If Peter or I had gone out with the wider settings on the 104cms the rear would have been so slidey it would have been impossible to keep it on line. The shorter wheel-base gave him a *hell* of a lot of grip in the corners so his settings went wider and wider.

"His kart was the same length from bumper bar to bumper bar as the rest, but what they did was move the rear axle 3cm forward, and in doing that they redistributed the weight. The seat position is the heart of the kart. He liked it like that because he always used it like that. In Jesolo, when he went on to two wheels and into the fence, it was because he was using the short-wheeled kart. I don't know why he liked it like that. Probably his style of driving. Even now you get people wandering round the paddock watching what others do then setting up their karts the same as the fast boys do. It is wrong. Everybody has his own style of driving to get the best out of what the kart can give him, and that is what Ayrton was doing."

You see it for what it is: not copying the fast boys but going his own way.

Parilla says that "Ayrton's speed was difficult to believe. The frame would jump like *this* or like *that* and he would stay full throttle. That's something natural, absolutely natural. It is true he liked the wide setting and this was, I would say, five or six years before anybody else discovered it was what you needed. When a race started he was immediately quick. I remember once at Jesolo he pulled far away from everybody in the first lap and in karting it's usually only one or two metres.

Lotus, boom, 1985.   Not with him. It came from the setting that he had and the power
in himself that he had. In karting there was no comparison with
him, no comparison, like he proved later in racing cars."

The 1980 World Championship was at Nivelles, Belgium, which de Bruyn
describes as "one of the most complete tracks: fast but with slow parts and very difficult because you can't have gears on the karts, you know, so to go fast round these
slow corners wasn't easy."

However serious on the track, it could be mildly chaotic (and in retrospect amus-
ing) off it. *Karting* reported that "the hopeful programme spaces for Mexico, Peru
and Uruguay failed to materialise and there were many attempts to slip drivers into
other countries at the last minute. The angry parents of a Dutch driver made an
enormous scene when he was denied acceptance as a Japanese. The two countries
who got the most extra drivers were Switzerland, using tiny Lichtenstein as a cover,
and Germany, with Israel as their B team."

Mike Wilson was not among the 104 entries. "I'd had an accident about two
months earlier on one of those little mopeds which everyone knocks around on in
Italy. I fell off it and although I was getting better I had a cough and chest prob-
lems." De Bruyn did compete and so did two future Formula 1 drivers, Stefano
Modena who won the Time Trials section (Senna tenth) and Ivan Capelli. In fact
Senna spun in the Time Trials but recovered quickly. He was ninth after the Heats.

In the First Final, *Karting* reported that "Silva overtook Marcel Gysin
(Switzerland) with the Brazilian waving his fist, apparently over baulking by the
Swiss. Meanwhile Fullerton now had the lead followed by Silva and Gysin. The
front eight were condensing into a solid column and Gysin's thrust past Silva sent
the Brazilian spinning off." These many years later, Gysin can't remember the circumstances of the accident or when he first met Senna. He does remember a comradeship forged and united by desire. "You are rivals in this sport and you just want
to win. Our rivalry was not to the extent of killing somebody, but we certainly
wanted to win. That was of the utmost importance. I thought highly of him.
Although we were rivals, there were always small problems, not big ones, and we

were always rubbing each other up. I find it difficult to explain. It really was the little things.

"Before Nivelles, I'd never had an accident and it was what we call a *carambolage*, a coming-together. It was not a tragic accident, no bones were broken or anything of that sort. When I look back, Senna had to improve himself as a kart driver as we all had to improve ourselves. Apparently he was a loner. He might have belonged to a team but he remained a loner. He could not accept to be second or third. He wanted to stand apart from the others. Again, I find it difficult to explain what exactly I mean by a loner. He didn't like it when he couldn't be number one and he didn't show it but we all knew. If you even try and hide your disappointments it's quite something."

Clearly Senna had the primitive desire to win and it consumed him until he learned to bring it under his control and accept the inevitable in some races; but not many races, and not until he had seen what he could do in them. Across his career he explored the art of the possible and at crucial central moments redefined even that; but we're at Nivelles in Belgium and he's 20, perhaps a young 20, perhaps an old one. Only he could make such an evaluation of gathering maturity and he never will now.

Senna won the Second Final. He made "an attack on Gysin (in the racing sense) and took over the lead with a waved thank you." Going into the Third Final, and the rules the same as 1979, six drivers could win the Championship: De Bruyn, Gysin, Jorg Van Ommen (West Germany), Alan Gates (South Africa), Senna and Fullerton. At the first corner de Bruyn and Gysin were together, a fractional gap from Silva and Van Ommen (*Karting*).

De Bruyn remembers that "I took the lead in the beginning and after some laps Gysin overtook me but I did not try and fight with Gysin because I knew Senna was just behind and for sure it would be a hard race.   *Dust storm, 1985.*

My decision not to do anything was based on the hope that Gysin and I would pull away from Senna and we did by 50, 60 metres."

It was a risk because, as *Karting* pointed out, "if they stayed in this order Silva would be the Champion. De Bruyn, however, took back the lead and the front pair separated away from Silva, who had earlier chopped Gates." So de Bruyn took the Third Final and the Championship, Senna second overall. *Karting* reported that "Silva had come close to getting the title and was less than happy at coming second. How he must have wished that Gysin could have stayed in the lead for the last few laps!"

De Bruyn says that "afterwards, Ayrton was disappointed but every driver is like that. It was especially true in his case because he'd lost it the year before as well. Now he'd had to win the Third Final or me not win it." In fact Senna could have taken the title by finishing third, provided de Bruyn didn't win. "Ayrton had had the pressure of six drivers being able to take the Championship, so he was disappointed, sure, but that's normal."

BELOW All hands to the wheel (John Townsend).

BELOW RIGHT Senna with Jackie and Paul Stewart at Monaco, 1986.

In 1980 the South American Championships were in Uruguay and Angelo Parilla went there. "We had a good time, no, we had a *really* good time. Ayrton was one and a half seconds quicker than everybody else. It was a nice place, a nice hotel and we never went to bed before 4.0 in the morning! He had a number of friends with him, some from Argentina, some from Brazil, and he was enjoying himself." And here it was, the side of the man so few saw.

Senna was already thinking of single-seaters, the next step from karts although the missing World Championship gnawed at him.

74

Most unusually in a young, ambitious driver who shouldn't look *Dust storm, 1986.*
backwards, he'd interrupt his single-seater career in both 1981 and
1982 and return to contest the Championships. Moreover, in 1981 he'd do three
kart races and in 1982 he'd do two.

1981

Senna joined the Van Diemen team, based in Norfolk, and within a couple of
months had established himself as an outstanding driver in Formula Ford 1600.
Knowing eyes watched this unfold, among them Alex Hawkridge of Toleman who
quickly concluded that Senna was dominating the races as no man had dominated
races since Jim Clark. Small Formula 1 teams, as Toleman were, constantly scan
the horizon for potential talent because they don't have the budget to buy already
created mega-stars. Here was the talent. By his third race Senna was winning, the
adjustment from karts quickly and decisively made.

Senna brought to England his young bride Liliane (nee Vasconcelos de Souza)
who, it would seem, didn't like the food, the climate or her husband's total absorp-
tion with 1600cc Formula Ford cars. Senna never spoke about this and Liliane, who
remarried after the divorce and has two children, has never done either, so far as I
am aware. He did however confess to Angelo Parilla that he himself found "a big
problem with the weather and secondly the food was a big problem, too. He loved
the food in Italy, he loved everything in Italy. I know that staying in England was
particularly hard for him but he knew it was necessary and he did it." He remained
in England (though wintering in Brazil, of course) until 1985 through Formula Ford
1600, Formula Ford 2000, Formula 3 and Formula 1 with Toleman and Lotus.

For the 1981 World Karting Championship, held in Parma, the engine capacity

75

was increased from 100 to 135cc, an unpopular move. Certainly, de Bruyn says, Senna "did not like it. The other thing was that Dunlop tyres dominated. He could not beat the other Dunlop runners because he did not have the engine and I could not beat them

because I did not have the tyres. That is to say, I had good equipment but not the good tyres. Nobody knows this, but on the last morning he came to me and offered me his tyres – you weren't restricted, you could do that – to enable me to win. Unbelievable. He understood that he couldn't win, he understood that I arranged everything in my team myself against the big factories and, actually, he was a little bit in the same situation with DAP, a very small team. So he made the offer. I said, 'what is this?' He said, 'yes, I'd really like you to win more than the others!' He

> On the last morning he offered me his tyres to enable me to win

was like that and in other ways we were similar. He didn't talk all day, he was business-like, doing the things you should do, the things you have to do. It's usual that there is a certain distance between drivers because otherwise you cannot go for it 100% on the track with them."

Wilson says that "we started saying hello to each other in 1981 but only if we happened to walk past each other." Here are the distances. "When you're racing, whether it's karts or Formula 1 – whatever kind of racing it is – you can say 'yes, he's a friend' but really he's just a friend to say hello to because when you are on the circuit you don't have friends. Everybody's out there to win and you can't afford friends, you can't, you can't. You must not put yourself in a position where you think 'I'd better not overtake him because I know him so well.'"

De Bruyn gives another perspective. "At that stage in a driver's career you don't know how good they can be in a single-seater. I had a year in Formula Fords and I do know that when you arrange good things around you, and with the experience that you have in pushing yourself to win, then you can. I was not surprised by what he did in single-seaters, not at all. If you're good in karts, 99 out of a hundred will be good in cars, but only the *very* good ones – Prost, Senna, Mansell, Patrese – come to the top. In karting you have many good drivers but not so many extremely good ones." Overall in 1982: Wilson, Forsman, Ruggerio Melgrati (Italy), Senna.

MILESTONES THAT YEAR. Senna drove the Van Diemen in Formula Ford 1600 and, of 20 races, won 12 and was second five times. Towards season's end he won five consecutively and finished second in the last, at Brands Hatch. He had been to the familiar British haunts – Thruxton, Mallory Park, Snetterton, Oulton Park, Donington and Silverstone – but not yet driven abroad.

1982

He increased his reputation in Formula Ford 2000, the next step from FF1600, but these cars had wings and so could be adjusted: a significant difference. He competed in the Pace British Championship but also the European Championship. This took him to Zolder on 18 May, his first single-seater race outside Britain. *Autosport* reported that "on pole position, by a clear 1sec, was da Silva, his Rushen Green-run Van Diemen once again completing only a minimum of laps and being handily quickest in each session." *Autosport* added that "sadly" the confrontation between

Senna and Cor Euser, a Dutchman and reigning European FF1600 Champion, "ended almost before it had begun as da Silva's Nelson engine let go after only three laps of the race and he had to relinquish his lead to Euser."

It made Euser briefly famous. "I didn't even know the guy," he says, "because I wasn't that much involved in racing. To me it was just a hobby. I'd won the European FF1600 mainly because of my Dutch friends who arranged everything around me. I had a 1979 Delta and Senna had a 1982 factory Van Diemen. My car was prepared by myself and some truck mechanics! After I won at Zolder, everybody was stunned. They said 'how can you beat Senna?' and I said 'who is this guy? I don't even know him.' Ayrton came over and said 'terrific job.' That was the first time we'd met and the first words he spoke to me. My English was so bad I asked my mechanics what terrific job meant and they told me. The ice had been broken and we started to speak to each other in our bad English.

" I tried to get friends with him but he was a difficult person to form a relationship with compared to the other drivers from England. It was easy to do that with them but Senna was – how do you say it? – different. I raced for fun but it was his profession, his job. Maybe he deliberately didn't want to make friends with people. He was a little shy and there was a small group of people he did talk to. After the Zolder race he spoke to me because he thought I was something special – I'd won the race. He could seem a snob but if you spoke to him he wasn't.

"Toine Hezemins, who was a Daytona 24-hour winner and main

Ayrton Senna at play on water
(Colorsport).

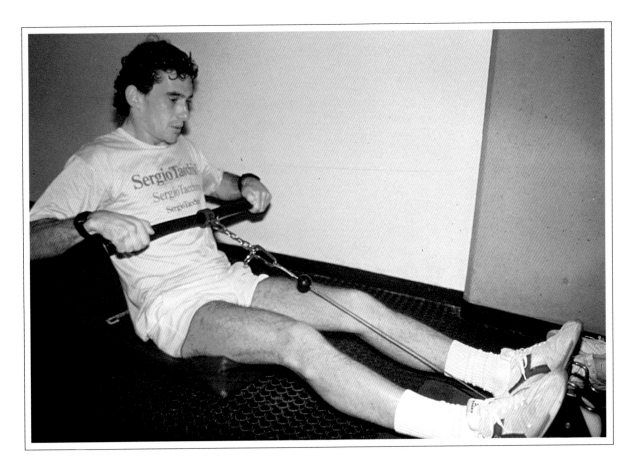

importer for Rotax go-kart engines for the whole of Europe, remembered Senna from karting and said 'you have to watch this guy, he's incredibly good.' I said 'well, I've beaten him!' Hezemins offered Senna £50,000 for a contract to be able to promote him and Senna wanted £75,000 or so and didn't do it. I was shocked to hear that type of money. I asked Hezemins 'why don't you sponsor me?' and he replied 'it's two different ball games the way he follows his profession and you pursue your hobby.'"

Ayrton Senna on holiday in Brazil, 1990. Some holiday (Colorsport).

Senna returned to Zolder for another European round on 9 May. Gilles Villeneuve had been killed on the Saturday, garbing this weekend in mourning. Senna had pole for the FF2000 race but, leading, made "a rare error and spun off into catch-fencing, throwing away an almost certain victory" (*Autosport*). The first six were: Huub Vermeulen, Jesper Villumsen, Rob Leeuwenburgh, Hendirk Ten Cate, Peter Elgaard and Max Busslinger. What dreams did these young men dream, and where are they now?

Senna retired in the fourth European round at Hockenheim and Euser crashed. "My car was parked in the open," Euser says, "and it rained the night before and we had to drill holes in the floor of the cockpit to let the water out. That night, too, some children were playing around the car and they changed the brake balance so badly that I had a very big crash on the first lap. That's how I went racing at that time. I got a new Delta which wasn't as good as the '79 and Senna beat me time after time. I always finished second. I didn't have the equipment to compete with him and his ability was a little bit better or his team were more professional. I don't

Senna, sister Viviane and a little shade.

say if we'd had the same equipment I could have beaten him, but I could have run closer to him. He wanted to have the pole and he wanted to have the fastest lap and he wanted to win the race and he wanted to win the Championship. I wasn't ready for that kind of thing. I was a hobbyist! We'd still speak but it was 'how are you?' sort of thing."

The World Karting Championships were at Kalmar in Sweden with, if you'll allow me the phrase, a one-legged final rather than the three. *Karting* reported that during it "the amazing Mr. Silva had made up half a lap deficit and then got all the way up to fourteenth which shows how he might have performed had he not had a puncture during his Time Trials." De Bruyn remembers "I went off, got back on the track and we did the whole final together battling for thirteenth, fourteenth place! I spoke to him quickly afterwards, he was already in Formula Ford 2000 and we talked a bit about that because I'd raced the Formula Fords myself in 1979. He asked me if I had any plans but I didn't have any. I'd only done the one year of car racing but at least I could speak to him about it."

Mike Wilson, who won in 1982, remembers the prize giving. "Obviously the first three were on the podium. The fourth driver came and shook hands with the first three and then stood by their side, the fifth man came and shook hands with the first four and so on and so on and it came to Senna, fourteenth, and he didn't shake hands with anybody because he was so upset. He really wanted to win the World Championship. At the time I thought the worst words you can think of, but looking back and knowing him more, knowing what kind of character he had, I'd have probably done the same

RIGHT The stress of 1987 (Colorsport).

thing myself if I'd been in that situation. It affected him so much not to have achieved it because he probably realised it was his last chance." And it was. The racing cars would become too important, too consuming.

RIGHT *Senna wins Monaco in 1987 but where are the people?* (Allsport).

De Bruyn started karting in 1968 and kept on until 1988. "After so many years of it, there are some karting drivers I have a hell of a lot of respect for. There was Francois Goldstein in the 1970s, Terry Fullerton, and then later on came Senna. Even though I was a little bit older than him, he was my generation, coming up at the same time in the international field. When you went to the races, he was the one to beat."

MILESTONES THAT YEAR. He drove Formula Ford 2000 for the Rushen Green Racing team, and of 27 races won all but six. The missing six? He retired in four and finished second in the other two. He also drove a Formula 3 race for West Surrey Racing at season's end, and won that, too. Anyone will tell you that motor races are maddeningly difficult to win. He seemed to find it maddeningly difficult not to win. And Championships. He won the Pace and the European.

1983

Euser describes Senna as "already a superstar" by 1982, albeit in junior racing formulae. This season, Senna's reputation broadened because his struggle with Martin Brundle for the British Formula 3 Championship moved to intense and combative proportions. Euser raced Formula 3 and found Brundle more remote than Senna "and Brundle speaks good English! I don't know why Brundle acted like that but probably he wanted to win as badly as Senna did and it's a question of keeping the distance with your opponents. That's what I have in mind when I say that. *If I speak to someone they might get information out of me and that's why I don't speak to them.* If you push somebody off the track and he's your friend he will be your enemy after the race, simple as that. We are all human beings but that's a calculation you have to make."

In mid-July Senna drove a Formula 1 car for the first time at Donington, which then measured 1.957 miles and took around a minute to cover. (It has since been extended, by the addition of the Melbourne hairpin, to measure a Grand Prix distance of 2.5 miles.) At the time, Frank Williams explained the background: "He came to see me a while ago, asking for advice, saying that everyone was offering him 400-year deals and so on, the usual stuff. I told him that I couldn't really advise him but that if it would help him to get the feel of the thing, he could have a run in one of our cars whenever it suited him. I wasn't acting philanthropically but I hope in the future he'll remember we treated him fairly."

Reflecting in 1995, Williams says: "After the first few laps it was obvious he was very talented, oh sure. In 21 laps he got down to a time which was about a second quicker than Jonathan Palmer (the team's test driver) and a second is a big difference over the 60-second circuit. He stopped and said 'I think the engine's going so I'd better pack it up.' The engine showed no signs of distress although it was sent for a re-build. I really think he said what he said because he was pressing on too hard – there were a couple of pictures taken at the time of him braking into the chicane with his left wheel half off the ground. I think he felt he should slow himself down by stopping! He was very good but I didn't come back to the factory and say to Patrick Head 'we've got to get this guy whatever happens.' Maybe that was an error . . ."

The revealing aspect, surely, is not that Senna instantly made a Formula 1 car go fast but that he couldn't find a balance between wanting to make it go faster, knowing he could make it go faster and yet fearing that he might not be able to cope if he did. That's only my speculation, of course, but he'd proved something else to himself. He could handle the ultimate level of racing cars, and handle it well.

MILESTONES THAT YEAR. *Driving for West Surrey Racing, Senna locked into the season-long battle with Brundle (Jordan) for the British Formula 3 Championship. Senna won the first nine races but Brundle, with Eddie Jordan persuading him Senna could be beaten, took it to the final race at Thruxton, which Senna did win.*

1984

Senna joined Toleman but drove two events outside Formula 1 which, in retrospect, assume particular importance because they demonstrate the scope of his abilities, something unseen since karting. Chronologically, Senna made his Grand Prix debut in Brazil on 25 March but the turbo boost pressure failed after eight laps; he ran to the end in South Africa on 7 April, sixth and his first point; ran to the end in Zolder on 29 April, seventh, subsequently hoisted to sixth when another car was disqualified; did not qualify for Imola on 6 May – a row with Pirelli kept Toleman off the circuit on Friday and Senna had a misfire on the Saturday.

A week after Imola, Senna took part in the inaugural race at the 'new' Nurburgring with each competitor having a Mercedes 190E. A strong field had been assembled, including Lauda, Reutemann, Keke Rosberg, Watson, Denny Hulme, Scheckter, Jack Brabham, James Hunt, John Surtees, Stirling Moss, Laffite and Elio de

Senna and Nigel Mansell head to head in Spain, 1987 (Colorsport).

Angelis. Here would be the conjunction with young Senna watching on the wall at Interlagos in 1976. An experienced sportscar man, Reinhold Joest, watched – fascinated. "They all had the same cars, normal road cars. Senna came, drove, won. He had a feeling for every car. I think he was the greatest driver I have ever seen, yes, absolutely, 100%." After the 12 laps (54.504kms):

1   Senna 26m 57.78s (121.286kph)
2   Lauda 26m 59.16s
3   Reutemann 27m 01.47s

How seriously all the competitors took this race is open to doubt and some were celebrity entrants as celebrity entrants should be: Moss had barely driven competitively since 1962, for example, and the Grand Prix career of Surtees ended in 1972, but there is no doubt that Senna took it seriously, saw it as a way of proving and promoting himself in such company. If he could beat *eight* former World Champions, that must mean something must it not? *Autosport* reported that Senna held the lead to the end "despite a determined challenge from Lauda, Watson and Scheckter." You'd better believe it: resisting strong challenges.

On 3 June, Senna finished second to Prost in the Monaco Grand Prix in a storm. Prost toured gesticulating for the race to be stopped while Senna caught him at an amazing rate and would have won if the race hadn't been stopped but continued for another lap. At one level Senna was angry to be robbed of what he conceived as his first victory, at another he realised that such an heroic failure brought him goodwill, admiration, sympathy and recognition. Later he spoke to Angelo Parilla.

Parilla: "Ayrton, the first 10 laps were bad. What happened?"

Senna: "The car was impossible to drive, there was too much power (in the wet) so I turned the turbo boost down. The more I turned it down, the better the car drove. At the end of the race, the boost was totally closed. No boost at all!"

In July Senna drove his only World Sportscar event, for Joest Racing. "I have a friend who knew Senna," Joest says, "and this friend said 'give him a chance, he wants to drive one time in sportscars' so that was the whole thing. I had never met him before. He came to the Nurburgring and I found him a real gentleman. He was 100% intelligent and not only in car racing but also in other points. You could talk with him politics, religion, a thousand things. He knew what he was talking about. He was also very sensitive. He came, saw the car and watched the car."

He'd partner Henri Pescarolo and Stefan Johansson. In second qualifying it rained and Quentin Spurring wrote this in *Autosport*: "Joest Racing lost its way in the morning session with the Le Mans winning 956B, over-experimenting with the settings. Johansson and Pescarolo monopolised the car in dry practice, leaving new recruit Ayrton Senna to learn the car in the afternoon. Until then, Ayrton had never driven a closed racing car in his life and had not even sat in a Porsche 956. After his first lap in the car, he was back in the pits asking for directions around the cockpit dials and switches. After that he settled down, finding the car much lighter to drive than he had anticipated. Soon he was showing the almost uncanny smoothness and consistency for which he is becoming known in Formula 1, and it was he who set the respectable (seventh fastest) wet session time."

> He realised that such an heroic failure brought him goodwill

Senna joins Marlboro
McLaren and
concentrates on every
detail.

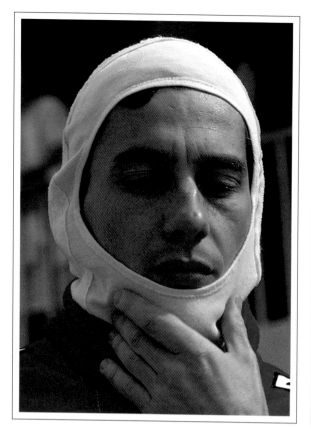

Preparing, 1988.
(Colorsport).

Joest says that "sure there was a big difference between a Formula 1 car and a sportscar but the 956 and the 962 (which another team, Skoal Bandit, ran at the Nurburgring) were, I think, the best sportscars in the world at the time. They had a lot of ground effect and so on. They were heavier to drive but the ground effect was the same. In feeling, the Formula 1 and sportscars were nearly the same. Senna was quick immediately, absolutely."

Spurring wrote that "the interesting Johansson/Senna/Pescarolo combination had worked the delayed Joest Porsche nicely into the top 10, but a lot more time – a crippling eight laps – had been lost when the clutch packed up. Now the car was running in a distant twelfth position, and, in common with several others, it was getting water on the electrics." It finished eighth.

"We had problems," Joest says, "and the drivers couldn't use the full turbo boost. Senna went on the outside line to overtake another Porsche and that was very impressive but, you know, when it's raining it's sometimes better that you don't have too much boost. After the race, Senna spent three hours with me and he gave me a list of 30 or 35 points, saying 'OK, you need to change this, you need to change that.' Some were small things and some were bigger things. It meant his life was his job and that was automobile racing." Those who disliked Senna, or called him arrogant, would see this unique de-brief as another example. He'd driven only one race in the Porsche and yet sat down and told its owner what was wrong with it. I don't think that's true and I sense Reinhold Joest doesn't, either. Senna was simply good enough to know this car (and perhaps *any* car) could be improved and felt it a duty not just to say so but point out how.

Ordinary people don't do this. Ordinary people can't do this, even if they wanted to. (Not much later, Senna confided to Angelo Parilla that "it was my first and will be my last time in sportscars. They're too big, they've too much weight, I don't like those.")

During 1984 Senna, who was involved with a watch company, went to the annual Swiss watch show in Basel and during this visit had a long lunch with journalist Roland Christen and a couple of other people. "We were able to talk properly," Christen says, and thereby hangs a tale. Senna did not forget Christen.

Meanwhile, Parilla says that "as soon as Ayrton went into Formula 1, that first year with Toleman, he discovered Formula 1 was a different story. And he didn't like Formula 1, he didn't like anybody in Formula 1 – so he had to make another face to show to the world. When I saw him being interviewed, it was not the same person that I knew. But if he came to Milan and stayed a few days with me or my brother he was the same person again. I asked what happened and he said 'I hate Formula 1 and all the people in it.'"

He'd had a hard season, and this may have coloured his views: not just 'losing' Monaco but the row in late August with Toleman when he told them he was leaving for Lotus. That emerged at the Dutch Grand Prix, Zandvoort, and for Monza two weeks later Toleman took the car off him, refusing to let him drive as the only punishment he would understand. Instead Senna went to see the Parillas. Angelo says that "he came to us three or four days before Monza and stayed. We said 'we can take you to Monza' but he said 'no, I don't want to go to Monza. I'll watch the race on television.'" In fact Senna did go to Monza, and tried to defuse the row by saying that all he wanted to do was drive and not have any more "aggravation." Toleman, the punishment over, gave him the car back for the last two races. This does not alter the central truth that all racing is hard – we've already seen the distances kart drivers maintained between

Precision, even in the rain.

OK boys, fire her up.   themselves – and that Senna had always been something of a loner among other drivers in the junior formulae. But Formula 1 is hardest of all. In what it does to its own people, it can be merciless, no sentiment, no prisoners. Curious. Senna could be merciless but he was unafraid of sentiment. We shall see.

John Love worked for Toleman. "We were quite close, because he lived in Reading with Mauricio Gugelmin and Mauricio's wife Stella, and I lived at Newbury. I didn't usually work on his car because I was doing tyres and composites and fabrication. In fact I did work on it once and that was at Zandvoort. A team-member's father died and he had to fly home. Ayrton was very young when he came to us and he was self-opinionated and a lot of the team took, well, not exception to that, but they felt that he was an upstart and nobody really talked to him much. He could appear bloody-minded and didn't seem interested in other people's opinions. To me, he was more a friend. I think people thought he was an upstart because they didn't really know him at all, most definitely.

"Even when he was so young, he knew exactly what he wanted and where he was going and, because of that, he had this air of too much confidence. People didn't like that. He could focus absolutely on one thing until he had overcome it and had it under his control. He certainly had two faces (but was not two-faced: that's a clear distinction). He did have a good sense of humour and so on but if you only saw the implacable face you couldn't judge that there was another one. Most people saw him at circuits or in the factory, where he was always deadly serious. At home he was completely different. There was only once when I remember having a joke and fooling around and that was at Zandvoort on the Thursday morning. I was chasing him round the paddock trying to kill the little bugger! I can't remember what he'd done.

"When it was to be announced that he was joining Lotus he did warn me in the morning that there was a load of crap going to happen in the afternoon. After that, Toleman wouldn't let him drive at Monza although he showed up at the circuit. Then he went back to Brazil. I had to go to his house every day and pick up his mail and send it on.

"He and Mauricio and Stella were all very close. To my knowledge, he never really watched any other driver racing except Mauricio. Again at Zandvoort, I remember after the Grand Prix there was a Formula 3 race and he stayed back for it, he sat on the wall and watched Mauricio do the whole race and Mauricio won and he was absolutely delighted. They were very, very close.

"In English, he understood more than he could speak. If it was something to do with the car or the racing he explained himself well, but if you were having a normal conversation that's when he would struggle; but he never forgot, never forgot. I always used to get a Christmas card and a birthday card from him years after he'd left Toleman."

When Senna journeyed to the Toleman factory to say a final good-bye in winter 1984 he wept. He always seems to have found leaving difficult. Gordon Message, who worked for Toleman remembers "he came down to the factory to say goodbye and he was very emotional. He knew everybody there because he'd jog or cycle to the factory regularly to see what was going on. He obviously had to go to Lotus but that didn't lessen his emotion. Maybe

BELOW LEFT Senna wins Belgium from Alain Prost in 1988 – before they fell out.

BELOW Words, with Pino Allievi.

Senna wins the San Marino Grand Prix, 1989. Tamburello is just ahead, just out of sight.

in later years he hid that side of him because he may have thought it made him vulnerable. Some drivers do feel like that. I didn't start going to the races in 1984 until the French Grand Prix at Dijon (fifth race) because before that my job was to make sure the cars were ready to be transported to the races. It meant I only got to know him in the second part of the season. I found him intense, very intense – in the way that Michael Schumacher is today, but maybe more intense than Schumacher."

MILESTONES THAT YEAR. With Toleman, and in his second Grand Prix – South Africa – he finished sixth. The sheer physical effort of 72 laps nearly overwhelmed him. Autocourse wrote that "once he had taken the flag, Ayrton relaxed and his hands fell from the steering wheel. It took all his efforts to regain control and he had to be lifted from the car once he reached the pit lane." His second place in the storm at Monaco, his fifth Grand Prix, echoes still. In the Championship he had 13 points, the same as Mansell who he was replacing at Lotus. Mansell went to Williams.

1985

In the winter of 1984-85, Senna, Gugelmin and Stella went back to Brazil, leaving John Love to go round to their house and "fire up the Mercedes which Ayrton had bought. He'd left it in the garage. I'd take it out for a drive to keep it in running order. It was a new Merc and it was his pride and joy – he'd bought it with his own money and although the family were rich, buying it himself meant a great deal to him."

And Senna joined Lotus. Bob Dance was then the team's chief mechanic. "Toleman was a small team and he had his sights set on bigger things. Lotus were

92

strong and during 1984 he decided Toleman wasn't quite the place he wanted to be. He was very keen to join us and of course we were very keen to have him, too. He had obvious potential and Peter Warr (running Lotus) was no fool. He picked a good man. I'd met him before at the Formula 1 races and he seemed a friendly sort of chap."

In those days, Formula 1 had a traditional pre-season testing session in Rio in February so, as Dance says, "we started life with him out in Brazil. He was down to earth and pleasant and his family were pleasant. We met them and his younger brother was around, his sister not so much. He did the testing and he was impressive considering he'd just joined us. It's easy to forget that he hadn't won a race yet and we really didn't know, and it is 10 years ago that we're talking about.

"What I found *immediately* impressive was this: we had Renault engines and we had the Renault engineers with us and a lot of little crystal display units had been taped in the dashboard area reading off about 10 things the engineers wanted to know. Bear in mind it was his first run in a Lotus. He said 'you see all that there (the displays). Don't expect me to come in and tell you what all of them are saying because I can't. But what I can do is tell you what half are saying on one lap and the other half on the next lap. Is that good enough?' He was already off and running.

"At the end of one afternoon, I said 'give me a lap in your hire car' and he took me round. He was on home ground, of course, and he said 'you see this section here, if the wind is blowing in a certain direction' – left to right, or whatever it was – 'that really makes you move across the track, you have to watch out for that.' It was obvious to me he was very astute and he thought about it all, every aspect of it. Then, on the other side of the coin, he was also a good sport with the lads. There

He didn't cover a lap at Paul Ricard in 1989. The transmission failed.

was more practical joking then than now. Lotus was very strong under Peter Warr, good morale, and Ayrton didn't escape the odd practical joke, but he also came back with practical jokes as well. He played a trick on me." And here it is:

Senna: "Have one of my sweets."

Dance: "What have you done to them?"

Senna: "No, no, nothing, they're good. Have a sweet."

Dance: "OK, I'll eat one, no problem."

It was a mistake.

"It made all my mouth blue," Dance says, "and when I went to pee in the toilet for the next few hours I peed blue as well. It was hilarious. Yes, we used to have some fun with him. He took all the boys out down the coast, he said 'I'll drive, I'll take you.' People don't visualise this, don't visualise him like this. He'd eat with us and that sort of thing. But as you come up in your career – and it seems particularly so in Formula 1 – there's more and more media hounding you and your life ceases to be your own. All the time, you tend to have to go into hiding. You want to sit down in a restaurant and eat with your friends but you can't: people wanting to know if there's any chance of an autograph, people wanting to talk, people wanting you to speak to other people (hence the attraction of the Romagnola in Castel San Pietro). In the end perhaps it overwhelms you a bit. I think he did take a decision to be two people: the private person and the public person, yes I think he did.

"He was very much a flyer of model aeroplanes and he'd bring his kit along. When he'd done his day's testing, he'd go out onto the straight by the pits and go flying with his models. He was very good at it. He could throw them around the sky. In Brazil, he'd chase the buzzards with his radio models or he'd get one up around the local microlite boys! It's fairly laid-back over there and they enjoy themselves."

Awesome Eau Rouge at Spa, more awesome in the wet.

That test session in Rio in February 1985 wasn't all so innocent. Senna and Mansell (then Williams) had a disagreement on the track, Senna claiming Mansell baulked him, Mansell explaining he was on a fuel economy run and if he'd slowed it would have wrecked the figures. Later in the day, on the last corner, the disagreement became physical. Senna struck the rear of the Williams, was airborne, landed heavily and damaged the Lotus. Senna said "I was much quicker than he was. I'd been trying to get past for half a lap. I'd tried one side then the other. When I went through down the inside he just chopped across my nose." To which Mansell said: "The first thing I knew was when I felt this big bang at the back. I'm in Brazil, and he's Brazilian. The back of my car is damaged, the front of his car is damaged. I rest my case."

This is a tantalising glimpse of the future because in the years to come they would know other, much more important crashes and both men would measure their willpower as well as their nerve against each other.

The story of the Portuguese Grand Prix at Estoril, second of the season and run in "diabolical" conditions is hallowed ground in motorsport. Senna had pole from Prost (Marlboro McLaren). On the parade lap Mansell and Pierluigi Martini (Minardi) spun. At the green light, Senna seized the lead and moved away from de Angelis in the other Lotus.

Lap	Senna	De Angelis
1	1:52.748	1:55.398
2	1:46.338	1:46.259
3	1:44.693	1:45.515

While Senna continued to build on this, the treachery of the conditions is revealed by a list. Philippe Alliot (RAM) spun off, lap 3; Riccardo Patrese (Alfa Romeo) spun off, lap 4; Martini (again!) spun off, lap 12; Berger (Arrows) spun off, lap 12; Rosberg (Williams) spun off, lap 16; Mauro Baldi (Spirit-Hart) spun off, lap 19; Prost spun off, lap 30.

Deep into the race – on lap 43 of 67 – Alboreto (Ferrari) moved into second place but 58.066 seconds behind Senna who, you'd have thought, would now cruise home, only increasing his pace if Alboreto mounted any sort of threat from the distance. Wrong. Alboreto did cut the gap to 55.433 seconds in another couple of laps. Senna went quicker than Alboreto for each of the next 10 laps, increasing the lead to one minute 12.639 seconds and when, on lap 56, Alboreto responded by cutting it to one minute 10 seconds Senna promptly accelerated again, forcing the lead to one minute 17.203 seconds on lap 60. *Then* he eased off, winning it by 1:02.978. It was devastating.

Nor had Senna forgotten Roland Christen. "A Japanese friend was starting 350cc racing in Japan, a bit like the kind they have in California. The cars look like racing cars. He wanted publicity for this and was producing a brochure. He needed a foreword from a Formula 1 driver. I wrote the foreword, wishing the venture well, but the idea was to get a driver to read it and if he agreed with what I'd written, we could use his name. At Monte Carlo during the Grand Prix I approached several drivers and they wanted money, some as much as $10,000 – just for reading a foreword, saying 'yes' and lending their name to it. One driver even referred me to his business manager! I began to get a bit desperate and we thought we'd have to pay. I decided to approach Senna – the great, upcoming Ayrton Senna – and I was prepared to go to, I think, $20,000. He didn't ask for money at all! He read it, approved it and said 'this sort of thing is good for the whole sport, our whole sport. I'm happy to be asked.'"

Toleman were bought out by Benetton and raced no more after 1985. "Just after Monaco in 1984," Love says, "Toleman got Michael Turner (a leading motorsport artist) to do a water-colour of the finish of the race. All you can see is Prost and Senna, everything else grey. Ayrton signed it. When Benetton took over they had a clear-out and I got the water-colour. I've still got it. It's funny-peculiar because I'm not the kind who keeps racing memorabilia and after 22 years of it this is all I have."

RIGHT Sometimes his face betrayed something close to physical pain (Allsport).

MILESTONES THAT YEAR. Senna's first F1 pole, and win, at Estoril. Seven pole positions in total and a further win, at Spa. The Championship: Prost 73, Alboreto 53, Rosberg 40, Senna 38.

1986

By now, Senna was close to being a Championship contender. Peter Warr recounts a revealing anecdote about the second Grand Prix of the season, the Spanish at Jerez. In qualifying Senna had an unassailable pole time of nearly a full second over Piquet as the second session neared its end. Senna did his lap and Warr said *OK, that's pole, you might as well get out of the car, no point in having another go.*

Senna insisted he wanted to stay in the car and did stay in it, eyes almost shut, for about a quarter of an hour. Then he announced to Warr that he would like to go out again because he'd been playing and re-playing laps in his mind and was convinced he could do a certain time, which he named to the fraction. Warr (wise in the ways of motorsport and actually a fan – if I may put it like that – apart from being a leading player) understood the nuances of the moment, understood that this is how a real driver behaves: you take the maximum from the car and, if you feel you haven't done that already, something inside you compels you to try again *for your own fulfilment.* And if a driver is not fulfilling himself in a car, what is he doing there? Warr ordered new tyres to be put on the Lotus, out went Senna and came back having done exactly the time he said he'd do.

Incidentally, it is this sort of thing which gets a team solidly behind the driver. They slog and labour to create a fast machine – an intricate, time-consuming and fraught activity – and the driver repays them by making it the fastest machine on the track. *He fulfils them as he fulfils himself.* Incidentally, also, this pole position (Senna 1m 21.602, Piquet 1m 22.431) was the hundredth by Lotus and Hazel Chapman, Colin's widow, was there to present Senna with a cut-glass trophy. He handled the occasion with his accustomed ease and sincerity.

"I think," says Bob Dance, "there was a danger we were going to lose him at the end of '86. I think he felt Lotus weren't good enough for him – in the sense of where he wanted to go. At the time we weren't looking as good as McLaren and he was setting his sights higher still. Lotus was not progressing, it was stagnant, shall we say. I believe what kept him with us for '87 was the active suspension we'd have. He thought it might give him an advantage over the rest and he put a lot of effort into it. He could tell you what the car was doing anywhere on the circuit, he could talk for as long as you liked about what his car was doing in a race. He would watch the race afterwards on the TV in the motorhome or in the hotel and he'd analyse his own performance, tell you what he thought of his own performance here and there during the race. He was very critical of himself."

MAIN PICTURE Imola, sombre and shadowy, 1991 (Nigel Snowdon).

BELOW A new team-mate in 1990, Gerhard Berger. Here they are in Hungary (Allsport).

RIGHT Senna wins Phoenix from Prost — now Ferrari — in 1991, and they were sworn enemies, weren't they?

Lotus had produced a prototype 'active' suspension in the early 1980s: computer technology allows the system to give the car a level ride. Peter Wright, the Lotus Technical Director, would say "we can take information from up to 20 different sensing systems at the rate of just over half a billion inputs per lap."

RIGHT *"There's definitely something wrong with this car. Wonder what?"* Senna in Canada.

MILESTONES THAT YEAR. *Eight pole positions, two wins, fourth in the Championship (Prost 72 points, Mansell 70, Piquet 69, Senna 55).*

1987

A young man from Sao Paulo, Rubens Barrichello, had a problem. "I was trying to get into the World Karting Championships," he says. "The karts were the thing Ayrton liked most all the time. That's why he had a circuit built on his ranch. My father rang him to try and get some help in understanding about the World Championships better because up to then I'd only done the Brazilian and South American. Ayrton was a great help. He phoned his old team, DAP, and I raced for that team. At that time, I was becoming a professional driver in karts, well not exactly a professional but I'd been racing them for six years, seven years. I met him when I went to Rio and he was testing for the Brazilian Grand Prix and I had some pictures of us taken together. He was a big hero of mine, for sure. By 1987 he'd already done things that nobody could imagine. He'd raced in Portugal and won (in the storm, 1985), he'd been on pole in Monaco, things like that so yes, yes, he was a person that every driver would like to be: not just if you were from Sao Paulo but the whole of Brazil."

By 1987 he'd already done things that nobody could imagine

During this testing Senna tried the Lotus 'active' car and felt it had such potential that the team decided to go whole-heartedly with it for the season and built three cars instead of the one originally envisaged.

In Formula 1, Dance insists, "it's fair to say we got the feeling that he wasn't happy with his results. That was not by any means down to his driving. On occasions, our car was unreliable and it wasn't a Championship-winning car. He could see greener grass as other teams got bigger. Lotus didn't get bigger with them. If you go to Ketteringham Hall (the Lotus base) now the race shop is virtually the same as it was in say 1980, but if you go to Williams or Ferrari or McLaren they've come on in leaps and bounds: the number of staff employed in development and testing, their equipment, everything you can think of. They've had millions and millions pumped into them year by year. That isn't obvious at Lotus and that's one of the reasons why it's gone down.

"When Ayrton left Lotus, he didn't come and see everybody because, unfortunately, we'd dropped him right in it in Australia. Adelaide is very heavy on brakes and we did all the usual stuff with larger ducts, putting on a flexible tube to get more air to the brakes. At the end of the race – Ayrton finished second – we were disqualified for over-large ducts, so he went off in a huff. Basically, it was because we had really let him down, I guess.

"How do I equate Senna with Jim Clark? Oh dear (chuckle). You have to equate them in their different eras. Clark could drive and win in virtually any car. Senna

Prost and Senna declare peace, Hungary 1991 (Colorsport).

didn't have that opportunity, so we only really saw him as an open-wheeled racing car driver (long pause). He had a reasonable mechanical knowledge and I think his model planes helped him in that. Clark had a reasonable mechanical knowledge, not a great knowledge. They were both (pause) . . . yes, intelligent young men. They had the desire to win. Coming second wasn't for them. When Senna was preparing to do a qualifying run, he'd watch his TV monitor, his car would be ready to go and he would decide for himself when it was time to go out. You knew he was going to qualify first, put the car on pole. That was the object of going out in qualifying. He expected 100% from the people who worked with him and he always gave 100% himself. He wasn't likely to have off days, even though he was a Latin. Some are very temperamental. I didn't class him as that type of driver. Clark was the same. In their respective eras they are equals, if I can put it like that.

"What is *it?* It's mental and physical condition, it's a natural ability. What makes a good pianist? What makes a good artist? They've that little extra, whatever it is, but it takes them to the top. As racing drivers, they have perhaps that little bit more daring but they know they can push that little bit further because they can control their situation. They have a very fine balance. Usually the quick men are good in the wet. Senna's second race for Lotus was in terrible conditions at Estoril, diabolical afternoon, cold, miserable, standing water. He had one 'off' but he didn't go off to the point of losing direction across the grass: he still had the car heading the right way and he wanted to win. It's the will to win, isn't it? He should have been an astronaut or a test pilot because of the involved work you have to carry out, not just a driver. He was capable of testing military aircraft, land them, tell you exactly what was going on, how they handled, everything."

MILESTONES THAT YEAR. One pole position, two wins, third in the Championship (Piquet 73, Mansell 61, Senna 57).

1988

So Senna joined Marlboro McLaren to partner Prost. (This ultimately degenerated into mistrust and rancour, hence the symbolic importance of what happened at Imola, 1994.) Senna won San Marino and led Monaco where he lost concentration and crashed into the armco just before the tunnel. Jo Ramirez of McLaren has recounted how he contacted Senna in Senna's Monte Carlo apartment five hours after this and Senna was still in tears. The Ramirez anecdote is well known but stands in amazing juxtaposition to what follows.

"What special personal memory do I have of Senna?" Pino Allievi of *La Gazzetta dello Sport* muses. "I have a memory of a man with two personalities. The year he crashed at Monaco he had invited me to have breakfast in his home on the Friday. I was there, I think, from nine o'clock until eleven thirty and I came to know a different man. That apartment was not, as you might imagine, typically French, it was a Brazilian apartment put in Monte Carlo. I remember the colours, the pictures, the walls, the furniture, the carpets, everything was Brazilian. The maid, a black grandmother if you like, she was Brazilian of course. Senna lived very happily in that atmosphere and so we spoke freely, off the record.

"I gained a very, very good impression but of a man totally different than the man I knew through motor racing. Then the following day during second qualifying he was totally different again and that's why I say two personalities, a man with two faces. One was when he was absolutely detached by the motor racing. When he was on the track he was capable of   *Words, Monza (Allsport).*

hating people like he did with Prost, because with Prost it was hate. With Mansell it was the same situation, and with Piquet. When he was far away from motor racing he changed.

"The thing that I regret is that he never compromised between his private life and his public life. He could have been better-known as a *man*. The biggest effort he made in his life was to hide his true face. He was a nice man with a complex personality, with many complexes. In a way he was a bit like Berlusconi (Silvio of the ilk, controversial media mogul and mega politician) but in a positive, not a negative way: invented by the society of image. Like Berlusconi and other people in other areas – Enzo Ferrari is an example – he worked all his life to keep his face private, to promote his image. He was *obliged* to give the public a positive image of himself. He was up there on the screen and he was obliged to hate Prost, obliged to say nasty things about Mansell. He was like an actor on the screen. I think he was troubled, because he never had the courage to show the public his true face and that was his biggest limit."

In the car this limit did not apply and he won the Championship in Japan and promptly cried again, but this time for the other, happy reason. Prost has described racing against Senna in 1988 as "relatively sporting" and the Championship as "conventional." Prost points out that he scored more points than Senna but the rules were the rules. However, Prost claims Senna enjoyed unconditional support from Honda and, when Prost asked why, he was told that Honda preferred Senna's "Samurai" style. This became a problem, and one which Prost easily recognised, because he knew that each year in each team one driver would enjoy a psychological advantage over the other, even when the

Words, Spa (Allsport).

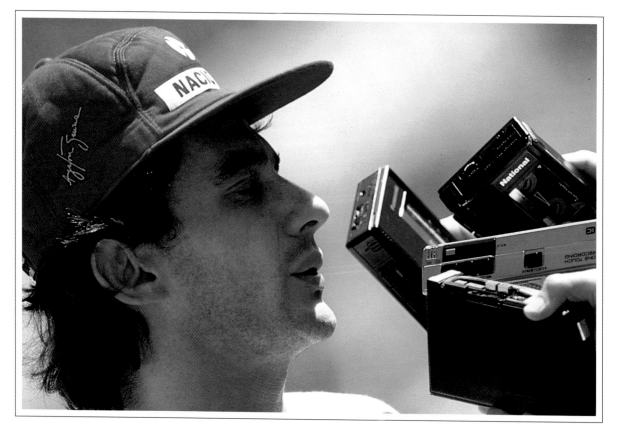

team was scrupulously fair about equal treatment in equipment. *Peace, Estoril, 1991 –* Prost concludes that the real importance of this can be expressed *with Riccardo Patrese* by a percentage: 80% of doing well is mental. (Nigel Snowdon).

Certainly, in its early stages, the Prost-Senna relationship did appear conventional. I remember tackling them on it at Silverstone and they made ordinary noises about each other, nicely couched in politeness and mutual respect. Publicity-speak? I don't think so. I remember it, however, for another reason. Senna was sitting on a chair in the Marlboro McLaren pit and I crouched on my haunches in front of him – to be at the same level – for the chat. Rather than stick my tape-recorder in his face I positioned my briefcase on its bottom, so it was vertical, and perched the tape-recorder on the top of it. As he answered the questions he stroked the briefcase with a foot, making it wobble and the tape-recorder wobble too, until it rocked to and fro but very gently. Just at the instant the tape-recorder *had* to flop over and fall from the briefcase he stopped, let it settle, resumed. Physically he had utter control. Not to mention that, simultaneously, he was smiling his *aren't-I-a-naughty-boy?* smile and answering my questions in what to him was a foreign language.

Mike Wilson won the World 135cc Karting Championships at Laval, France, (beating among others Peter de Bruyn and Lars Forsman) in 1988. "I went to Paris for the annual motor sports awards, and of course Ayrton was there because he'd won the Formula 1 World Championship. I went up first to get my trophy, because they started with the smallest category, which was karting. When I was walking back with it he stood up from his table, came over, put his arm around me and said 'well done. I see you're still winning!' I said 'yes I am, but obviously it's not as important as yours although it is important to me.' He said 'the really important thing, whatever you're doing – whether it's karting, Formula 1, whatever, even playing cards – is to be the World Champion because that means you are the best in the world. Even in karting it is a great, great achievement.' That was nice, very nice."

MILESTONES THAT YEAR. Thirteen pole positions (a record, beating the nine of Lauda in 1974 and again in 1975), eight victories (a record, beating Prost's seven in 1984 and this season of 1988, and Jim Clark's seven in 1963). Because a driver could only count his 11 best finishes from the 16 rounds, the Championship finished Senna 94 but 90 counting, Prost 105 but 87 counting.

1989

On Saturday, 26 August the Lotus cars of Nelson Piquet and Satoru Nakajima failed to qualify for the Belgian Grand Prix at Spa. Since the team began, at Monaco in 1958, this had never happened before. The great days had gone and that Saturday afternoon you wondered if there were many days of any kind left. The last man to win in a Lotus was Ayrton Senna, USA-East Grand Prix, Detroit, 21 June 1987. In all, he'd driven 48 times for them, 16 poles, six wins, exactly 150 points. Since he'd left, Lotus had won 35 points, no wins. As I write this in spring 1995 Senna remains the last man to win in a Lotus and, the team now merged with another, it may stay like that for all time.

Senna, of course, had pole in the Marlboro McLaren Honda at Spa but rather than celebrate that he spoke with undisguised sadness about the decline of Lotus. "I had good times but also bad times. There was a lot of frustration but I had my first pole position there and my first victory there. I know most of the people and most are good, professionally and personally. I think to see a team with such a name going down, as it has the last two years, is sad. And today, when neither Lotus has qualified, is particularly sad, but in this business you get what you ask for. If you make wrong judgements, wrong decisions, sooner or later you pay for it. Maybe today is one of those occasions." You could not mistake his sincerity, how he felt laboriously for the right words, how softly he spoke them. The sentiment, you see.

He'd never deliberately distanced himself from the Lotus personnel. "We saw him to speak to," Dance says, "and he would always talk to you, same as usual, but as more and more media people were after him he got more and more shut away. The best chance one had to talk to him was if we were doing testing and, in fact, that was the last time I did talk to him, the testing at Estoril in '93. Just a chat. 'How are you doing?' sort of thing. He'd always have words for you. Away from all the pressures of the races, he was a very human sort of chap."

Mike Wilson won the World Karting Championship again, this time in Valence, France. "This was on a Sunday and I returned to Italy (where Wilson lives) on the Monday. *La Gazzetta dello Sport* said only 'Mike Wilson wins World Championship in France.' Senna must have seen this because he telephoned Pino Allievi and said 'all the Italian journalists think they are the best in the world, especially in motorsport, and you write practically nothing on somebody achieving a world championship for the sixth time.' In fact, Allievi phoned me on the Tuesday and asked me if I could give him an interview. I did that on the Thursday in Milan, and on the

Friday I got half a page in the *Gazzetta*. I found what Senna had done for me not just so nice but absolutely incredible."

Allievi is unsure about this call, although he did interview Wilson. What Allievi does remember is that, at a subsequent Grand Prix, Senna said to him, "Why don't you give more space to karting? It's a very good sport and you have a lot of Italians in it."

Either way, the episodes are surely instructive. Senna cared.

At Estoril during the Portuguese Grand Prix, Mansell and Senna crashed in circumstances of great controversy after Mansell had been black-flagged but insisted he hadn't seen it. That is to say, Mansell ought not to have been on the track, making the crash even harder for Senna to take. On the following day Senna gave an explosive interview to Allievi which reverberated into wild headlines all over Britain when it had been relayed from Italy. The gist: *Mansell put my life in danger.* I was curious about the circumstances of this interview because, in its time, it represented much more than just another Formula 1 explosion.

During practice Senna told Allievi where he was staying, with the Bragas at Sintra. "The morning after," Allievi says, "I went there with three other journalists and spoke with Braga, who told us Senna was still sleeping because they'd had a dinner the night before and it was a little bit early for him. I had a problem because I had to tell my newspaper what I'd be writing so I went back to my hotel in Estoril to do that. From there I also phoned Braga and Senna was now having lunch. I left my number and around two o'clock Senna rang me. I did the inter-

RIGHT The concentration which took him into another world. This is Spain 1992, but it could have been anywhere (Colorsport).

BELOW Insiders, outsiders, 1992.

BELOW RIGHT Words, Japan.

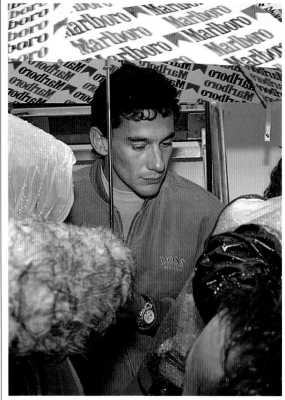

view there, on the phone. If he knew you and trusted you he would ring and it was really kind. We spoke Italian because he spoke it perfectly. He used the correct grammar and spoke it as well as the average Italian, he didn't make mistakes."

RIGHT *Fifth at Spa* (Nigel Snowdon).

Two thoughts: if Senna did trust you he'd talk and he knew precisely how to manipulate the media, in the sense that he understood the impact his words would have. He didn't pick up a phone and bleat and babble about injustices. He calculated *and you cannot misinterpret what I have said because I have selected the words with laboured precision*.

The Championship turned on Japan, where Senna and Prost crashed at the chicane, giving it to Prost and detonating another Formula 1 explosion. Some saw it this way, some that; some blamed Prost and some blamed Senna; certainly Prost blamed Senna and Senna blamed Prost. Ah, well.

MILESTONES THAT YEAR. *Senna took 13 poles and won six races. Prost headed for Ferrari to partner Mansell. Berger would come to partner Senna. The Championship: Prost 76, Senna 60, Patrese 40.*

1990

Senna gave an interview to Steve Rider of the BBC and was on his best, relaxed, whimsical form, even when asked the hard questions. I reproduce a fragment of the dialogue to illustrate that, gestures and all.

Senna: "Fear is an important feeling in your mind for self-preservation" (slow smile).

Rider: "Maybe you have less fear in a cockpit than other drivers around you?"

Senna: (slow smile, smooths collar of driving overall) "I don't know how much fear that they have. I know that I have enough to keep me in control and keep me as healthy as I am" (the smiles are included not because talking of fear amused Senna but because it was a way of normalising having to discuss it).

On 29 September he covered the 2.621 miles (4.218km) of Jerez in one minute 18.387 seconds to take the fiftieth pole position of his career for the Spanish Grand Prix. Nobody had been remotely near such a total before and that evening it looked like this:

Senna	50
Clark	33
Fangio	28
Lauda	24
Piquet	24
Prost	20

Yes, yes, there are lies, damned lies and statistics but there is no escape from the central truth that this league table is monumental and an authentic reflection of what Senna had been able to make so many cars do to reach the 50: Lotus Renault Turbo, Lotus Honda Turbo, Marlboro McLaren Honda Turbo, Marlboro McLaren Honda normally-aspirated. There'd been qualifying engines of 1000bhp-plus; there'd been a bewildering array of circuits – Mexico with its bumps, Monaco with its demand for absolute precision, Detroit with its manhole covers, Silverstone with its broad acres, the Hungaroring with so many corners it became a carousel, the full blast of Monza, the dips and rises of Interlagos. Each he had mastered.

Spain on 29 September was the same and starkly different. Towards the end of first qualifying, Martin Donnelly (Lotus) crashed with a force so great that he was wrenched out of the car and flung onto the circuit unconscious. Senna went to the scene to see for himself. The next day he pressed down whatever fear he may have felt and went for pole. The on-board camera recorded the lap, and re-watching it remains a startling experience. At one level it's almost brutal: the engine screaming, the corners rearing, the hands wrestling the steering wheel, the McLaren swallowing the circuit. At a second level it's calming because, in the midst of all this, the driver is *placing* the car and what seem wild moments on the rim of the possible are in fact predetermined. At a third level it is suddenly very, very frightening.

Rounding a right-hander onto a straight at maximum speed, the world juddering, the helmeted head bobbing, a spectre loomed: two cars – Piquet (Benetton) and Olivier Grouillard (Osella) – travelling comparatively slowly and having an argument about something. They were over to the left. Senna pitched the McLaren right and went round them, his closing speed so vast that in a milli-second they melted from view. What if he'd touched either of them?

Afterwards Senna was happy enough with the 50th pole but used his Anglo-Saxon on the two drivers. "That was totally unaccept-

BELOW The fruits of victory.

BELOW RIGHT The fields of defeat.

able." He added that he'd had to "hesitate on the throttle" when he saw them, otherwise the lap would have been quicker still . . .

Monaco, sun and shadow, 1993. Senna won from Damon Hill (Allsport).

In any qualifying session, watching Senna was awesome and fascinating. Those who worked with him try to explain it as best they can. He could divide his thinking into compartments: the weather, what the opposition had just done, the surface of the track, the time remaining in the session, how the engine was, how the gearbox was, how the balance of the car was, which set-up would be optimum. He could then bring all these factors from the compartments and make a complete, living picture of how he would exploit each factor and create a great harmony from them. If you saw him sitting in the car in the pits waiting to go out, if you looked carefully at his eyes, they were *studying the picture*. It is exactly what Peter Warr saw Senna — eyes half closed — seeing at this same Jerez in 1986.

It must be said that the Marlboro McLaren, though not perhaps the best handling car, was strong all the way through. The Championship, however, proved deeply unsatisfactory at its climax in Japan where Senna argued with officials about moving pole position to the clean side of the track and, when they refused, decided to let fate decide events in the first corner. He and Prost crashed and went off. All else aside, it gave Senna the Championship and provoked, yes, another detonation. Ah, well.

Berger proved to be a good team-mate and became a friend. Both he and Senna indulged in wonderfully disgraceful practical jokes against each other (recounted in my book *Gerhard Berger: The Human Face of Formula 1*) and both learnt from each other: Senna to be less serious, Berger to be more serious. Genuine friendship between rival drivers is rare and thus far Senna's partners — Johnny Cecotto, Johansson, de Angelis, Johnny Dumfries, Satoru Nakajima and Prost — had come and gone in various states of disarray. Senna *liked* Berger and Berger *liked* Senna.

MILESTONES THAT YEAR. *Hundredth Grand Prix (Mexico). Ten pole positions, six wins, his second World Championship (Senna 78, Prost 71, Piquet and Berger 43).*

1991

Owen O'Mahony started to work for Senna as his pilot, flying the HS125 (cost $8.5 million). "He'd got the plane at that stage but evidently he'd had problems with Brazilian pilots. He rang British Aerospace and said 'send an English one!' So I went out to Brazil. To be perfectly honest I wasn't really a Formula 1 fan but the name Ayrton Senna seemed vaguely familiar. *He's a driver, isn't he? I'm sure I remember that name from somewhere.* Prior to that I'd been in aviation for years, flying people like Idi Amin, but I became careful because you start wondering about the Robert Maxwells of this world and do you really want to be involved with them?

> ## We'd sit and chat in the plane for long periods of time about all sorts of things

"It took about six months for Ayrton to smile at me. After that, we'd sit and chat in the plane for long periods of time about all sorts of things. He was an endlessly fascinating man to talk to and it was endlessly fascinating to see his mind in operation. Mind you, it was never a quick brain, never ever a quick brain" (in that he thought carefully before he spoke: you cannot by definition exploit a Grand Prix car if you think slowly). Often, however, during long flights Senna would go into what O'Mahony describes as "brain shut-off. He'd listen to music or sleep." The eight seats on the plane could fold down into beds. "One thing I'd like to think is that I helped him with a sense of humour. I tend to go around seeing things in funny terms, or at least the funny side. In fact I taught him an expression which he later used against me, gave it back to me, he did. It was 'how long have you been working for me *not including tomorrow?*'"

Before O'Mahony, nobody had asked Senna if he'd like to have a go at flying the plane himself and Senna never did ask O'Mahony "can I?" They evolved a coded language with Senna wondering "what's the wind like at Faro?" which meant *I would like a go if it is safe to do so.* "Obviously," O'Mahony says, "you don't do anything silly like on the approach to somewhere like Heathrow, but Faro in the evening could be very quiet." Flying the HS125 Senna was "happy as a little sandboy and the interesting thing was that you only had to tell him something once. His feel was amazing.

"He didn't need the aircraft in the close season and it was kept in the UK. Occasionally I'd take people in it to keep it in working order, so to speak. It was funny because I took the ex-President of France, Valery Giscard d'Estaing, down to a weekend of shooting in Spain. Next time I was flying with Ayrton, he said 'how come you, with all your *mafia* (!!!) friends, can't get me a ride with Williams?!!!' It was at the time he was negotiating with the team (who of course had Renault engines) and we'd had a couple of clandestine meetings with Frank Williams. The plane could fly London to Sao Paulo direct, although I once did do it in two legs, stopping at the Cape Verde Islands (off the African coast).

"The effect Ayrton had on people was amazing. I've landed him at Sao Paulo airport and had to shut the engines off because people knew he was coming and they'd break through and run towards the plane." One time, by the way, Senna confided to O'Mahony that he didn't intend to retire until he'd won six World Championships – one more than the record, held by Juan-Manuel Fangio who O'Mahony describes as "Ayrton's hero."

MILESTONES THAT YEAR. *Eight pole positions, seven victories, third World Championship (Senna 96 points, Mansell 72, Patrese 53).*

1992

There's a lovely anecdote from Angelo Parilla, who happened to be in Brazil. The anecdote travels back to karting. "In concentration, the only person who was close to Ayrton was Terry Fullerton. I saw a television interview on Brazilian TV and the interviewer asked Ayrton 'who's the best driver you've ever met?' – thinking he'd say Prost or Piquet or Mansell, someone like that. Ayrton replied 'Terry Fullerton!' The interviewer said *'who?'* The fight between Ayrton and Terry had been something special all those years ago, an enormous story." Ayrton Senna had not forgotten.

There's a lovely anecdote from John Love, long out of Formula 1 but attending a test session at Silverstone. "I was just a face in the crowd." Love stood outside the Marlboro McLaren pit as Senna emerged from it in the car. It happens like this: always around the mouth of the pit were journalists, photographers and the curious simply wanting a look, wanting proximity. The driver, emerging, has a safe path through them because they stand back or they are held back, but the driver makes the car move at surprising speed and has already twisted it rightwards into the pit lane. He's thinking of many things, what he's supposed to be doing with the car, what the car is supposed to be doing with him, how this adjustment or that

The debrief in the motorhome. Michael Andretti is on the right (Allsport).

MAIN PICTURE *The first chicane at Monza, which isn't wide enough for both Hill and Senna* (Nigel Snowdon).

INSET *Silverstone, 1993* (Empics).

Tears, 1992.

will work: a different concentration to racing. Testing is a laboratory full of endless experiments, racing is their conclusion.

So he came out and twisted the wheel to take the McLaren sharp right along the pit lane and in the blurr of faces gaping, he recognised John Love – who he hadn't seen since 1985 – and waved a gloved hand to him. "Ayrton remembered, he remembered me."

How can a mind do this?

But he was only human, never claimed to be more or less.

In December, courtesy of Emerson Fittipaldi, Senna flew to the Firebird Raceway, Phoenix, to try a Penske Indycar. Rick Rinaman was there and I propose to simply let him speak. "I'm crew chief for Emerson. I had not met Senna and, of course, before you have a personal impression you take what you have heard or read. The papers over here had long written that he was a hot-head, temperamental when things didn't go his way, so that was my impression going in. It was my car that was being used – Emerson's car – so I had to work on getting Senna to fit into the tub, make seat belt adjustments and so on. The thing that surprised me so much was that the guy was a gentleman to everybody. He was professional, he made sure he went up and introduced himself to everybody there. It was quite an experience for us all. Nobody was left out. You didn't have to be high on a pedestal for him to talk to you.

"Emerson went out first and did quite a few laps and got some respectable times, he came in and then I put Senna in the seat. No, no, he hadn't had a seat fitting so he sat in Emerson's seat. The pedals, the seat belt straps were all different because he wasn't as tall as Emerson. I was ready to start adjusting everything to fit him but he said 'oh, no, that's OK, don't go to any trouble.' We put the seat belts on him

118

and they were loose. I said 'I'll just tighten this strap' but he repeated 'oh, no, don't go to any trouble.' He had to *reach* for the pedals – so we did very little to actually get him comfortable. He was going out to do some shake-down running to feel how the car handled.

"So out he went, warmed the car for a couple of laps, came back in and said everything was all right. Out he went again and stood on it for two laps – a track he's never been on, a car he's never been in – and in about three laps he was quicker than Emerson (chuckle). I mean, everybody was just in awe. Back he came and of course everybody, the engineers, myself, and Rick Mears (an Indycar great) gathered round the car to hear his comments on it. Listening to this guy explain what this car was doing was unbelievable. The guy was able to tell you things about what the car was doing that I had never heard *our* drivers explain before. He was telling us when the ground effects would give up, when the suspension was working and when the downforce was working. It was an amazing amount of information he gave to us in about five minutes. He left an impression on everybody there which was like *when are you coming over here?* (chuckle). He left, I am sure, with a good feeling in that you want to do something but you have something else that you need to finish first (the Formula 1 career). I would have bet anything in the world that the guy would have been over here doing Indycar within the next few years and he would have been outstanding, oh, absolutely. We talk about it nearly every day. We were talking yesterday (February 1995) about Senna and that test . . ."

MILESTONES THAT YEAR. One pole position, three wins, fourth in the Championship (Mansell 108, Patrese 56, Schumacher 53, Senna 50).

1993

Senna met Adriane Galisteu at the Brazilian Grand Prix in March. She was doing promotional work there and could barely believe it when he showed an interest in her; but he did. In her book, her account of their falling in love seems to suggest he was far from a playboy/ladykiller. On the contrary he proved to be a little shy and hesitant over their initial contacts. Bearing in mind he could have arranged 50 different 'dates' every evening *anywhere* if he'd wanted, the shyness and hesitancy are rather nice, aren't they?

"He used to call Adriane on the radio from the plane and I had to get the connection," O'Mahony says. "One time she was in New York and he rang the number twice but no reply, she must have been out. I said to him, 'Ayrton, this is love, isn't it?' He said *'hmmm'*" – which O'Mahony took to mean yes. "She was a lovely girl and I have a photograph of her and I cuddling. She was very tactile and I showed the photo to Ayrton. I said, 'there you are, this shows you she prefers older men' and he said 'Owen, I will remember this when it comes to your next contract!' Once at Monaco I said to him 'take all her credit cards away and don't give her any of your credit cards.' He replied that it wasn't a problem. 'She's the best girl I've ever found. All she wants to do is to go to McDonalds!'"

Barrichello, a fellow Brazilian, made his debut in Formula 1 driving a Jordan Hart. "My first race, Kyalami (also the first of the season) Ayrton came to me to say that if I needed anything I could go and ask him and he'd try and help. That was really good. I went once to him in Monaco because I didn't know the way round (no testing in the Principality, of course, because the circuit is on public roads, thus there is no chance to familiarise yourself until free practice begins) and we talked;

but he was a busy man so I never wanted to bother him. I think he liked me because he was so good to me and many times he helped in set-ups of the car, things like that."

At Donington, immediately after Kyalami and Brazil, Senna drove an epic race to win the European Grand Prix in wet-dry-wet-dry conditions and in a McLaren which did not seem capable of victory. Deep into that race Barrichello rose to second place which, in context, represented a feat as great as Senna's. "Donington was one of the races where I felt I was able to do something special. I had a great start," Barrichello says. "From twelfth on the grid I completed the first lap fourth and I felt at home in the wet. The conditions made my car more equal with the others and I was doing really well until I had the problem (fuel pressure)." Pausing briefly for another context, Barrichello had covered 31 laps at Kyalami (gearbox), 13 in Brazil (gearbox again) and thus when he reached second place at Donington on lap 49 he was into uncharted territory. "I understood that the gravity in Formula 1 is so big and you have to get used to it. You try to build up muscles doing exercises but the best exercise is in the car. That race my lower back was hurting but I was in there and I was concentrating on a finish." Barrichello held second place for seven laps before the problem. "It was very sad not to finish, especially with Ayrton on the podium. I didn't have a chance to speak to him afterwards but I saw the interview he gave to Brazilian TV and he was feeling sad as well that I hadn't been on the podium. Physically, you have to do at least a year (to be in shape to withstand the strains of a full race). You can finish races, you can smile, but it's *hurting*. It's not that easy and you have

BELOW Senna having a close look at Phoenix.

BELOW RIGHT Would you have gone in a road car with this man? Some did, but not always twice.

to work your mind as well as your body." Senna, at Kyalami in 1984 – his second Grand Prix – did the full 72 laps and was so exhausted he had to be lifted from the Toleman, don't forget.

There's another glimpse of Senna after the Donington race. "Usually I'd wait at the airport for Ayrton to come back," O'Mahony says, "and I'd try and watch the race on television, which I managed to do 99 times out of 100. However, if it wasn't possible and I didn't know when he did come back, you couldn't tell whether he had won or lost (he exercised absolute control over himself). I watched Donington on a TV in the control tower at East Midlands airport and I had a mobile phone. We were due to take off at 6.0 or whatever. The phone rang, hell of a noise in the background. It was Ayrton from the track. He drank very rarely and when he did drink he didn't drink much but he became *squiffy* – not drunk, just squiffy. 'Well done,' O'Mahony said, 'that was bloody amazing,' to which Senna said 'Owen, I think we'll go tomorrow, not tonight!'"

In September 1993 Senna took Adriane and competed in a kart meeting at Bercy, Paris. Philippe Streiff, a Formula 1 driver paralysed in a 1989 testing accident, had had the idea of creating a kart meeting to raise money for charity. Streiff "didn't really know Senna before my accident because I was competing at another level (he'd spent his career with mid-ranking teams, Ligier, Tyrrell, AGS). I do remember one year, after the Japanese Grand Prix and before the Australian Grand Prix, we went to Bali: Boutsen, Alliott and myself. We stayed at the Club Med and we arrived in the afternoon, he arrived in the evening. We threw a surprise party for him. He seemed very tired and while we were there he slept a lot.

> He drank rarely and when he did he became not drunk, just squiffy

"When I had the idea for the karts I got Prost to agree to drive. At Monaco in 1993 I went to the McLaren motorhome – I remember it so well – and asked Ayrton if he'd compete. He said yes he would and he also said 'I began my career karting and I'll probably end it karting!' No question that he wouldn't come because Prost would be there. We did, however, have a problem because Senna was with McLaren who used Shell fuel and Elf were our main sponsors – they'd come in with Prost. Senna's advisers pointed out that his contract with McLaren ran to 1 January 1994, 15 days after Bercy. I found a way round this. I spoke to all the people concerned and it was agreed that he – only he – would run with TAG Heuer on his kart.

"It was resolved only in early December. He was due before the FIA in Paris over the Eddie Irvine incident – when he'd hit Irvine, a silly matter really (after the Japanese Grand Prix) – and I was due to see him afterwards. The FIA meeting went on longer than foreseen and Julian Jakobi rang me to say Ayrton wouldn't be able to make our meeting. He did though manage to give a brief interview to *L'Equipe* that evening and they asked if he would be at Bercy. He explained the problem. I met him next day before he flew back to Brazil and he said 'yes, I am coming if I can.' When everything was sorted out I rang him in Brazil – it must have been midnight in Paris, nine at night over there and he'd just finished water-skiing – and it was on then. Because he would be coming specially, I sent him an aeroplane ticket but he never used it. He could have simply given it to a relative or a friend to use if he didn't want it for himself but, no, he didn't. He paid for himself, and none of the drivers were being paid for competing. This was for charity.

"When he arrived I explained that his French fan club had taken 500 seats and of course there would be the usual press coverage, which was important to the event. He was wonderful. There was no antagonism between him and Prost. They chatted about this and that, and I have some lovely photographs of them together smiling. In fact, when Prost won, Senna was applauding. The competition was on the Saturday and Sunday and Ayrton flew back to Sao Paulo that night. He was in the office at eight o'clock the next morning telling people how much he had enjoyed himself."

Mike Wilson attended Bercy with his son and daughter. "Ayrton and I spoke a bit but there were so many people round him all the time, young kids, even grown-up men asking for his autograph. I said 'it must be difficult to go anywhere' and he said 'yes, but you learn to live with this. It would be nice for me to walk down the Champs Elysees, just me and my girlfriend, walk down and do some shopping, but unfortunately it is not possible. I'd be stopped every five metres.'

"At Bercy each driver had his personal room upstairs where he could change. After the racing he called us up. He had three hats and he put one on me and dedicated it to me. He wrote on it *to Mike, with admiration. Ayrton Senna*. He gave one to my daughter which said *to Anna, with love* and one to my son which said *to Alex with admiration*. He also gave me a gold-plated key ring and that was touching. If people didn't know him well, they found it very difficult to understand how good a man he was. This was the other side of Senna that not many people saw. Since his death, there's been a lot on television about him and half the time I can't even watch because I get that feeling in my throat where you stop swallowing. I've three or four videos, one of which comes from Brazil, but I find it difficult to watch all the way through. It shows you the other side of him, when he was back in Brazil and he's playing with his nephews, he's out on the sea and he's smiling all the time and he's enjoying himself. Few people saw that side and that was the problem. I did actually know the other side of Senna. I'd go into the bar when Formula 1 was on television and people would say 'oh, Senna blah blah blah' but I didn't start anything because it would have been a continual argument. They didn't know what they were saying because they didn't know him at all."

Across 1993 Senna astonished by how competitive he could make the uncompetitive McLaren and arguably he had never driven better. What was it he had? Barrichello ruminates on that. "He would do things 100%. He would sleep with the car, wake up with the car, understand the car better than the others. He had good cars but he made them work well. He was quicker than every team-mate, the only comparison you can make. Sometimes Berger was in front of him but you have to say that in 100 times that was only 10 times. It was a natural speed, a natural *understanding* of the speed of the car and a great belief in himself. In Formula 1, you don't have just to be quick, you have to think, you have to finish and sometimes you have to take risks. He had the whole combination."

MILESTONES THAT YEAR. *Hundred and fiftieth Grand Prix (France). One pole position, five wins, second in the Championship (Prost 99, Senna 73, Hill 69).*

CHAPTER FOUR

A time to weep

*T*his is a direct sequel to the chapter "Cries from the heart" in *Ayrton Senna: The Second Coming*, published by PSL in 1994, the week before Imola. That chapter consisted of completely unsolicited letters from all over the world, sent following publication of my previous book on Senna, *The Hard Edge of Genius*. In quantity and content, they were unlike the postbags I had received for any other book. In an evocative, penetrating way they captured the impact he exercised on total strangers. I approached putting the chapter together with some trepidation because I'd never seen anything like it in print before and there was always the chance it would be mis-read, particularly by men. All those letters came from women. I felt, however, that no understanding of Senna could be remotely rounded off without the extent of the impact.

Since *The Second Coming* appeared – and since Imola – many good folk have said that the chapter struck a profound chord; and these good folk have grappled with their own emotions to try to evaluate the impact of the man and to accommodate the loss. I reproduce extracts of this grappling (it's the only word for it) with, in each case, permission. Some of the extracts are extremely personal and I offer my respect to those who have had the courage to let me reproduce them. All but one of the extracts are from women. Two of the correspondents asked for their names to be changed, for reasons I won't go into, and I've gladly done that. That said, their extracts are authentic and as written. The first requesting anonymity – I'll call her *CW – from Illinois* pushes the whole subject into broadened, unexpected directions.

"I occupy that world of the female auto racing fan which you seem to find so strange and fascinating. I have pen pals all over the world who are in the same situation. My American and Australian pen pals and I were all hugely affected by Senna's death but rather than wax poetic about the whole thing, we have either tried to define it or just turned our backs on Formula 1. The reasons for our reactions are twofold: first, Americans are pretty much shut out of Formula 1 and the simple fact is that Senna was a stranger to us. Second, American women, and to a certain extent our Australian sisters, know that women are every bit as capable as men of driving race cars extremely well but are prevented from doing so by the still-pervasive bias in the sport.

"I'm not saying there is no such thing as an American racing groupie, as I've seen

far too many of them at the track to make such a naive statement. In Brazil, things seem to be a little different from anywhere else in the world. My Brazilian pen pal was not a Senna fan, having instead opted for the Piquet camp, but since Ayrton's death she has written some very moving things. The most poignant of all was when she told me she prayed to Senna to help the Brazilian soccer team defeat Italy (of this more in the next chapter). Now I know why that final penalty kick went sailing up in the air like it did! But I would never tell her that joke, because to her this is serious, and praying to Senna for help is as natural as breathing. My Canadian pen pals (one male, one female) both went into denial about Senna's death and I have not heard from either of them since early June.

"Senna did have a nice body and, I'm told by those who met him, a lot of charisma. Some have even tried to tell me he was remarkably handsome, but I'll draw the line there. I'm sure that, faced with a female international racing star, at least some men would find themselves running off at the mouth. Definitely *Penthouse* magazine would be scrambling to find a nice photo of her, or some other blot in her past that they could bring her down with.

"What I'm saying is that I don't think this Senna thing (whatever it was) was particularly a female thing. I don't think it's something peculiar to women that some of us love dangerous men who would die for speed. Just look at all those female-in-danger movies and the fact that, while most real-life serial killers are men, most of them in the movies are women. All this tells me that there's a sizeable male market for images of dangerous females in peril. The difference is that when a man looks at a woman, she either becomes a sex object or nothing at all, but when a woman looks at a man he might become her son, her peer, her lover – but rarely nothing at all. To me the only really interesting thing would be to see how women would react to a female Senna. I think what we'll see is a feeling of comradeship and relief that one of us has finally made it. At least, that will exist unless she sells her boobs to *Penthouse* or flaunts her face in *Vogue*. The path this woman will have to tread in public will be 10 times more perilous than any she will ever face on the track. And when you think about it, it will not be entirely different from the path of Ayrton Senna."

This letter arrived at the end of July. In a subsequent letter in January 1995 *CW* added:

"A touching story may interest you about another pen pal of mine. She was an elderly English widow who adored Senna. She was never quite the same after May 1 (she was a feisty old devil before then, but afterwards she could just barely bring herself to answer her mail). By the time Fall came she was in failing health and she collapsed and died December 1. I can't prove that it was all because of Senna, but I do believe his death played some role in hers.

"Now I have a confession to make. I had my come-uppance a few months after writing to you when I was contacted by another Senna widow – an *American* (CW's italics) woman who was as obsessive about Senna as any of the women in "Cries from the heart". Previously I had chosen to believe that American female racing fans felt enough opportunity in their (everyday) lives that they would be less likely than others to succumb to obsession for a distant racing hero. But corresponding with this woman, along with my preliminary research for a book I'm intending to write about female racing drivers, has reminded me that I have been choosing to see things only in a very narrow range. Obviously it isn't only prejudice that is keeping women out of racing, it's the women themselves clinging to their old chains.

"I've become fascinated by the different faces Brazilian drivers show at home than they do in other countries. What got me going on this was Indycar driver Raul Boesel, who is everything Senna wasn't (except successful): handsome, mature, accomplished both on and off the track, likeable, homorous, a born diplomat. At least he is that way to the US public. My Brazilian friend tells me tales of Brazilian television appearances by Boesel which have been 'torrents of tears and volcanoes of emotion,' as they say. So how does this apply to Senna? I don't know, except that I have the feeling that Brazil saw him quite a lot differently than did the rest of us."

Not to mention that millions worldwide saw Senna as handsome, mature, accomplished both on and off the track, likeable, humorous and sometimes a diplomat, although we won't ask Eddie Irvine for his considered view on this.

We miss him so unbelievably much the pain sometimes feels like crazy

The obsession with Senna, and it certainly was and is an obsession, leads down another path. How was it possible that he exercised this impact upon people who didn't otherwise follow Formula 1, or were introduced to following it only because of his presence in it, or found a new meanings in Formula 1 through him? *Grietje Swater of Nieuw Vennep, Holland,* gave some of the answers in August 1994:

"Writing this I realise that I don't know how to go on. Only yesterday I said to my beloved man 'life without Senna!' We both loved him. Even still, there are moments in which I become aware of the fact that it hasn't sunk in. My brain knows but my heart won't accept it. We miss him so unbelievably much the pain sometimes feels like crazy. We started to follow Formula 1 on television, back in 1988, such a short time ago. We were dependent then on Belgian television and, although they tended to favour Alain Prost, we recognised Him immediately: his driving and equally his character.

"There have been moments in these past six years in which I jumped up in fright when something went wrong with him, but my heart iced when I watched him come off Tamburello. I didn't want to believe it, but immediately I knew that this was it. And at the same time it was like being in a dream, this can't be true, this can't be happening. I got this intense sad feeling in my body. I felt kind of sick and very weird. I don't like to believe in these sort of things, premonition or presentiment, I don't know which one is the right word but I think you will know what I mean. Although I tried to suppress it my body kept this awkward feeling. Like so many others, I had had the feeling that nothing could ever happen to him. I still catch myself for a second with joy looking forward to the next race, expecting to see him. I feel anger that there is nothing in the world to make this right, like one's own mother was used to making things right when you were little. It brings up feelings of intense loneliness.

"Ayrton Senna was an artist. He had an artist's character. He drove a racing car with a motivation comparable to people like Frank Zappa had, or Jimi Hendrix had, needing to make music. Nothing could interfere with this thing, least of all his own limitations! I make a distinction between people who are 'born' an artist and people who go to a certain building in which they are kept occupied by other people who are being paid to tell them what to do. And then, after a couple of years spent in that building, they get a piece of paper which says they have qualified to be an artist in something or other! These people I called skilled labourers. They are probably good in their profession – that's a matter of opinion – but they are not born artists.

"I name a few who were, not just Hendrix but Billie Holliday and Richard Burton. Unfortunately they lacked something which was of the greatest importance because they lost a grip of their lives. They didn't have this great instinct and analysing gift which Senna and Zappa did have, and were thus able to keep control. These artists do not need to be told what to do because they know exactly what they want and what is required to be able to do that. They need to develop themselves and they find a way to gain the necessary information. They have a great dislike of unnecessary information. They have a tremendous ability for analysing. They are consistent and able to concentrate on anything they do at a level most people cannot understand. They have a tremendous feeling of responsibility towards their time of life: you have this time, why waste it? They seem to have overcome the deep-inside feeling of uncertainty from which almost every human being suffers.

BELOW LEFT Phoenix, *afternoon.*

BELOW Barcelona, *afternoon* (Allsport).

"Their qualities make them often seem very demanding and are even called self-ish. It can be frightening for some people because it is very confronting. And yes, if you work with them they are demanding and give 10 times as much if not more – but selfish? Who was the first to see Rubens was all right? As Patricia Boutsen (wife of long-time Senna friend Thierry) said of Senna, and this is most significant: 'When things are going well you don't see him, but when the going gets rough he's there.'"

Now, for Senna as the conduit to seeing Formula 1 afresh.

Wendy Thomas of Gwent, Wales:

"I have been a motor racing fan for many years, but since the start of Senna's career it had a whole new meaning for me. I always go to Sunday school as I am a teacher there, and every Sunday when there was a race on at an early start-time the boys knew I would be racing (on foot) through town to be home in time to see the start. Many people cannot understand the admiration I had for him, although I never met him. I seemed to know what he wanted to do.

"Since Imola I have been devastated and feel so numb inside it is unbelievable. Afterwards I was trying to do a crossword (I can't seem to do anything properly since his death) and I had to look in the dictionary under the letter 's' and as soon as I opened the page I saw 'Senna' – definition, tropical plant. I couldn't believe I was seeing his name in a dictionary. On May 1 and May 2, I had many phone calls and visits asking how I was. Many friends knew I would be distraught. The ones who understand most were my son Stuart, my sister Sheena, and Elaine Linney, my friend. They were really kind to me, and my husband Alan, although I'm not sure he understood all the tears. I feel part of me has gone, and I don't quite know what to do."

Or *Jennifer Riley from south of London:*

"I am a Grand Prix fan. It all started in 1974 when I was taken to my first British Grand Prix, aged 18. I fell in love with the atmosphere, the noise of those fantastic racing cars driven by men who personified the ultimate in bravery. In 1984 I noticed a new young Brazilian driver, very good looking, slender and almost delicate, but possessed of a great self-assurance. It wasn't until the following season that I really began to appreciate his exciting driving style, now being shown to advantage in the beautiful black and gold Lotus.

"For nearly 10 years I watched him race on the Grand Prix circuits round the world and after the races I listened to his intelligent and articulate comments. With those intense brown eyes reflecting different emotions and his beautiful voice . . . he was an extremely charismatic man. I find it difficult to understand the attitude some people held towards him: the view that he was selfish, arrogant, cold, too aggressive in his driving style. I think these people forget that Ayrton was a human being and that all human beings express some of these traits."

Yes: never claimed to be more or less.

Carolynne Kristina of Doncaster (who corresponds regularly, is a most sympathetic reader and even calls her cat 'Harry', an early Senna nickname):

"My first recollection of Ayrton was 1984 when he drove the Toleman in the Monaco Grand Prix. My husband was there watching it live, so you might say this is where my interest in Formula 1 and Ayrton started. There is just no-one to replace him. I am sorry to say this, but I find no excitement watching the other drivers and even Schumacher leaves me cold. I could never contain my excitement when Ayrton raced – my family gained much pleasure watching me watching Ayrton! I quickly got carried away. I even threw a cup of coffee in the air when he made his famous 'mad dash' at Donington in 1993. I was banned food and drink after that until the race was over or Senna retired. I still feel sad and I still cry. I feel this man gave me so much. I have been going though a divorce – it is finally ending. My passion for Ayrton and Formula 1 helped me get through my bad marriage. I really do have so much to thank him for but, alas, I never will be able to."

Suzuka, late afternoon (Allsport).

The immediate aftermath of Imola left many emotionally adrift.

Lyn Patey of Leamington Spa in January 1995:

"Even after eight months, I still find it difficult to talk about or fully accept what has happened. I can stand back and give a cool, analytical account of the immediate effects – the extraordinary reaction of people around me, the letters, telegrams and messages of sympathy and support that I received from the most unexpected quarters. In those first awful, unreal days I was subject to the same sort of support that my mother received when my father died. It was unbelievable – and fascinating from a detached point of view. What I can't do is delve too deep into my own, still chaotic, feelings."

Pam Jones from Sutton Weaver, Cheshire, on 3 May 1994:

"It is two days since Ayrton was taken from us and the emptiness is as acute as when my own mother died. I find myself constantly asking: how am I going to survive without him? Of course I never 'had' him in the conventional sense of the word but he was so much a part of my life that the loss is acute. When the news came through on Ceefax that he was 'clinically dead' I almost collapsed.

"Like many women who have written to you, I find — I say 'find' rather than 'found' deliberately because he will always live in my memory and on video — myself similarly attracted not just by his physical beauty but also by his genius, his dedication and his humanity. You always know that however well he managed to do in a race, he had always done his best within the limits of circumstances and machinery. Therefore one never felt let down or cheated by him, because you knew that no one in the world could have done any better. I will always remember Silverstone two years ago, when Mansell mania was at its height. It was Friday qualifying and I was standing at Woodcote, watching him. Among all the Mansell fans it took some courage to wave to Ayrton. One felt everyone was accusing, everyone was thinking 'how unpatriotic' but I was acknowledging my hero. I *had* to do it."

Jenny Coles of Sheffield in August 1994:

"For years I was amazed as well as outraged at the sheer amount of attacks on Ayrton, not only on his conduct as a driver but also as a man. Then I realised that, of course, nearly all motor racing journalists are men, and therefore would never have the same understanding of such a special person as Ayrton, partly because of simple male jealousy (what man wouldn't be frustrated by another who was so attractive to women and so damn good at such a male orientated sport?) but also because only a woman could have the intuition to really understand such a complex man.

"I had been eagerly awaiting your second book and it duly arrived in the post (ordered pre-publication) on Saturday 30 April. I read the last chapter first as that was what I had been most interested to see, and the quotes in it, in "Cries from the heart", so echoed my own feelings that I felt strangely subdued for the rest of the day. And with the terrible events of the Saturday afternoon, I decided to save the rest of the book for another day. Then came the next day . . .

"It is difficult to describe my feelings after it became clear that Ayrton wasn't going to survive. I was so shattered I couldn't even cry for a couple of days. I grieved for him as I would for someone close to me, and I find it so difficult to explain to people that I have given up trying.

"What was the overwhelming attraction of this man who I never met? His looks, of course, played a part. I'm a happily married woman of 35 but he was the most gorgeous man I have ever seen and every move of his oozed sexuality (and yes, my husband knows my feelings). Those soulful and intelligent eyes were incredible, and yet conveyed a real sense of vulnerability. One of your correspondents mentioned the deep emotion of a loving mother, and I think that was the key. The relationship between a man and a woman is based on the physical protection that a man can give a woman, whereas the woman provides emotional support for her man, the same as she would for her child. Some men more than others have the qualities which bring out this protective instinct. Ayrton had these in abundance, even without being in physical contact with him. This partly explains why so many women were prepared to jump to his defence after one of his so-called misdemeanours; any mother will excuse her child anything.

"For my own part, I have had some awful personal problems over the last few years, including not being able to have my own child, and so I have maternal instincts in abundance which needed a direction and Ayrton became the recipient, for the reasons I have already mentioned. But his attitude to life, and his determination to succeed, were qualities which I came to admire and aspire to during periods of absolute despair in my life.

"The Irvine affair produced a barrage of criticism about Ayrton's volatile nature, and yet all these same people had relentlessly gone on about how 'cold' he was as a person. They failed to appreciate that he was in fact of a typical Latin temperament but was intelligent enough to want to control that part of him and present a cool, calm demeanour to the world; just occasionally it would get the better of him. He wasn't perfect. That was part of the attraction."

Yes, never claimed to be more or less.

At this point we'd better have the words of a man, *Marcel van der Nol of Oudewater, Holland*, and for a reason:

"In '92 I was there when he had his fight with Mansell in the closing stages of the Monaco Grand Prix. I watched them on the big television screen by the harbour for most of the time, saw them come out of the chicane towards me and on to the Swimming Pool. Senna won and on the big screen it looked like he sprayed the Moet and Chandon over our heads. This   *Estoril, evening* (Allsport).

is something to tell my grandchildren about (although it's a little early for that because I'm only 21). Later that afternoon I saw Ayrton standing in the red and white McLaren motorhome. He looked shy, almost afraid of the people outside who yelled his name: Senna, Senna, Senna . . .

I understood the true greatness of his soul, if not his earthly persona

"He drove away on a little scooter and I ran beside him, hoping he would stop for an autograph. He couldn't of course. He sounded the horn and slowly accelerated towards the Swimming Pool. I was tired, but I could touch him. I am sure he must have been afraid because of the huge crowd around him. I would have been, too. He smiled to the fans and I stopped running, watching as he disappeared. A German came towards me and asked *'war das der Senna der an uns vorbeigefahren ist?'* Yes, it was Senna, I said, and he smiled. We both knew we had seen a living legend. He'll become an ever-increasing legend and I'll always miss him."

Interesting, isn't it, that the women dreamed of Senna in a distant, untouchable way but the man tried to touch him and get his autograph?

One aspect of the mystery of distance and proximity – of being with him or *feeling* being with him though you never have been – is explained in a single paragraph from *Renee Sharp of Newcastle upon Tyne:*

"I understand completely what you (the author) meant when you said you knew Ayrton well, and yet not at all. I do not wish to unduly flatter myself, but many people feel that way about me, too. I am also Aires, born on March 28 (Senna on the 21st) and share many of the characteristics of Senna. Maybe that's what drew me to him so completely. I knew how he felt so many times."

Whether you believe in premonition is your business, but I ask you to approach the next extracts with an open mind because the writer is not, as she explains, a star-struck teenager who has taken leave of her senses. The extracts are from *AD of Adelaide, Australia,* who also wished to remain anonymous.

"What I am about to write may disturb you, but I do not mourn the death of his physical body. My heart goes out to his family and those who love him and feel a sense of loss, but I view the situation from a different perspective, that of truth. (In an earlier letter) I made reference to the fact that his career was only the training ground for what would come later, and when the training had finished it would end. If you take careful analysis of the personality and attitude of Ayrton during 1994, you will see a changed man, a man who knew his earthly life would end but one who, like most of us, did not want to face this prospect. However, the script unfolded as it was meant to.

"In early 1990 I was given a vision. Not a dream. There is a difference, because in a dream one is asleep but a vision is given when one is awake, most probably so that one does not forget it. The vision was of Ayrton Senna's body lying in state and the world mourning. In 1990, what had this man done to deserve such a thing? And, in truth, did his earthly feats up to his death warrant the burial he received? He was buried like a king. Most odd, wouldn't you say? But for me, who had travelled a strange journey since 1990, I understood the true greatness of his soul, if

not his earthly persona, and to me he received the honours and respect he deserved; but I am biased.

Ayrton Senna, 1988 (Allsport).

"The spectacular way he left this earthly life has had a profound effect on mankind, far greater than what is deserved by someone of his profession and achievements. Not that I dismiss them, but it is out of all proportion to the personality we saw on earth. He has touched people in a way that goes far beyond that of a man who was a Brazilian racing driver, even if he was three times World Champion. The reaction to Ayrton's death is totally illogical. In our subconscious mind is a knowledge which far exceeds our conscious knowledge (thank goodness) and it is this subconscious knowledge about the entity who lived as Ayrton Senna which has flowed to the surface and manifested itself in a quite extraordinary outpouring of grief. In Australia this has been out of all proportion to his following as a racing driver. I have watched as people who didn't know much about him openly wept and genuinely mourned his death.

"It is obvious this rather unassuming young man has been able to reach deeply into the subconscious of mankind and has left a void in people's hearts which they are at a loss to explain. As I said, the subconscious knows, the conscious denies."

There can be no doubt that Senna's faith found a very deep resonance in some who followed his career. *Laura Giglio from Milan* writes:

"Towards the middle of 1993 my son made friends with some Christian Evangelists and decided to go to their meetings. As a consequence he started to talk of the Bible and the real existence of God in our lives. From then on, I began to look at the events which tied me to Senna from a different angle. Anytime I asked 'my' God for a sign, it came. I didn't yet know that Ayrton was experiencing the same faith that I was approaching and it was only later that I discovered it. In Ayrton, I've found the co-existence of the two most important laws of God: love and freedom. These are the most precious gifts I could receive to fill my life with. I've asked Him to let these feelings live in me because I cannot see how a normal human being could match Ayrton Senna. I cannot rationally say it will last forever, but as long as it does I'm safe.

"I know it's foolish to feel myself so tied up with someone who was a total stranger, but I felt as if a part of me had died in that crash at Imola. Immediately I took all the things concerning Senna, put them in a drawer hidden from sight and decided never to take them out again. I avoided watching television or reading newspapers because I knew they would speak of the accident but at the same time I felt frustrated because, in acting the way I was doing, I was losing the chance to see Ayrton again. What was even more painful was the fact that, except for my children, the people around me could not understand my reaction and, I guess, they considered me a little bit out of my mind. I'm not completely free of feeling desperation (in January 1995). My daughter feels this, and any time that I come across something unexpectedly which is connected with Senna, she hopes I haven't noticed it so that it doesn't hurt me again. I'm collecting magazines with articles on him but I cannot open the pages straight away. I must gather all my strength if I want to read them."

The last extracts come from a woman who simply signed herself *Mrs G. Robey, writing from Swadlincote, Derbyshire.*

"Although I never met him, I feel in a sense that I knew him, if you understand. I watched every race that he competed in, and in every race I felt as though I were in the car with him. He seemed to have a personality which drew you to him. This man, who so many people could not understand and could not get through to, was I think deep down a very lonely man. I shall never forget that fatal day at Imola. My family and I had just sat down to watch the Grand Prix, as we always do, when his car went off and crashed into the wall. I kept shouting 'get out of the car Ayrton, get out'. The tears were streaming down my face. The pain I felt, the sheer panic and distress, were intolerable. My husband kept telling me that he would be all right but this made no difference to the anguish. I ran upstairs and prayed to God to let him live. The next few hours to when they announced that he was dead were the most unbearable I have ever experienced in my life. I loved that man so very much, so deeply, so truly.

"I wrote to Frank Williams and asked if he would be kind enough to send me a photograph of Ayrton, and to my delight I received a picture of him. I cherish it. It has pride of place at the side of my bed, so that the last person I see at night and the first person I see in the morning is Ayrton. I miss that man with all of my heart and always will. There is one wish that I have in my life. It is not a big car, a big house or a lot of money. It is to go to Brazil, to the Morumbi Cemetery, to pay my own last respects. I know it will take me a long time to save to go, because my husband is disabled and we do not receive much money, but dreams do come true and I know that one day I shall go."

CHAPTER FIVE

And a time to every purpose under the heaven

Ayrton Senna believed in God, and it was not just an aspect of him but essential to him. We have reached a fundamental. A casual spectator of his career might well wonder how a practising Christian could nurture a hatred of a competitor, as Pino Allievi (among many others) insists he did with Prost, or indulge in such uncharitable (let's say) actions on a race track as crashing and bashing those who stood in his way. No doubt he'd have countered by pointing out that a Grand Prix is not tea with the vicar and, if you want to win, these things will happen; if you don't want to win, knock tremulously on the vicarage door and go in there instead.

It's not necessarily a contradiction that in the heat of battle and its aftermath he reacted like a racer, just a racer, because he regarded his faith as something *overall* but not perhaps dictating every single action of his professional life. The aftermath of the 1993 Japanese Grand Prix illustrates this. He felt Irvine had been naughty (let's say) during the race and he sought him out and cuffed him. That's a racer's reaction. When Senna had calmed, he defended the logic of why he'd done what he'd done but confessed that he knew the cuff was completely wrong. He didn't use the word immoral but he might as well have. That's a completely different reaction and one which moves back under the umbrella of the overall, his morality re-established.

I propose to give you other illustrations and leave the conclusions up to you.

In early 1991 Professor Sid Watkins's two stepsons had an interesting but surely unreachable notion. They were at Loretto, the Edinburgh boarding school, and from time to time Loretto had a guest speaker on a Saturday night. The stepsons invited Senna. All else aside, the week of the requested lecture Senna was testing at Estoril, itself enough for him to mutter a polite 'thanks, love to but I can't'.

"Much to everybody's surprise, Ayrton accepted," Watkins says.

After testing on the Friday he took his own plane from Lisbon to Heathrow, where he collected the Professor and his wife and they flew on to Edinburgh. "He stayed at my house, which is in Coldstream. On the Saturday I took him to lunch, a pub in the Borders where nobody recognised him and that pleased him immensely. Incidentally, when he used to come and visit me at the hospital where I worked in London we'd nip out for the odd Chinese meal in the East End. There again, he was very rarely recognised. One or two people would look at him as if it couldn't be true! And since I didn't call him by name they assumed it wasn't true."

Watkins did something else this Loretto weekend. Discreetly he telephoned the museums officer of Berwickshire District Council, who run the Jim Clark Memorial Room in Duns, not far from Coldstream. It was closed for extensive refurbishment. Watkins explained to the officer, Jeff Taylor, that he had an important guest who didn't want to be named but who would very much like to have a look around the Room. Gently, Taylor coaxed the name out of Watkins and opened the Room specially. Taylor explained to me in an earlier book (*Champions!* by Christopher Hilton and John Blunsden, MRP) that "without being disrespectful to Senna, he didn't seem in any way overawed by all the trophies because he'd plenty of his own, and after all, trophies are trophies. He was much more interested in what Clark was like. I imagine they were the same type of people, quiet, reflective. I looked at him and I thought: this is a very controlled man."

At Loretto, Watkins says, "it wasn't really a debate. Ayrton gave a talk. He'd borrowed a slide or two from the Jim Clark Room and gave his talk. He took questions for 20 minutes or so. He was absolutely super. He also had some photographs taken in the Loretto chapel, where there is a plaque to Jimmy Clark (a pupil in the 1950s). Afterwards, we went and ate supper in the headmaster's quarters with some of the Sixth Form and some of the older boys who had been invited as well. The Bishop of Truro (Michael Ball) was there and he and Ayrton got into a nice little chat about religion because, of course, they were on opposite sides of the wall: Anglican and Roman Catholic. However, they got on very well. Then Ayrton had to leave and I took him to the airport so he could fly back to Portugal. The next day, the Bishop was giving the sermon at the school and in opening it he said how very impressed he had been with Ayrton and that he felt outclassed as a preacher . . ."

BELOW Oh, that's what happened.

BELOW RIGHT A rare study. He didn't often disport himself like this in public.

The Bishop of Truro, a delightful man, concurs. "I may well have said 'compared with the faith I met last night, I shouldn't be standing here at all!' Ayrton Senna struck me as forcibly as that, yes, definitely. He came over as a great sort of wave. His personality was attractive and he had a lovely sense of humour. Though we did talk about the faith, I'm not one of those people who finds it easy to talk about unless it's spiced with humour, and he had that ability, too.

"In every way he was unlike so many people who are rich and famous and powerful. He actually did take an interest. He still retained the power to relate to other people. Without any patronisation or anything like that he remained interested in people as people, and that is rare. Loretto have some notable figures every so often to give a talk on Saturday evenings in term time and they were lucky enough to get him. The great thing proved to be not only how good he was in the talk but in the way he answered the boys' questions. He was scrupulously honest and didn't spare himself along the way.

"For instance, they said 'what about your relationship with Alain Prost? What *is* your relationship with him? The newspapers all say you hate each other'. He replied 'well, of course, I can't offer an opinion about what Prost thinks of me but, as far as I am concerned personally, our relationship is very good. But he is a competitor on the track and there we go all out to get each other'. He added 'Prost's remarks about me are entirely up to him'. They challenged him about his relationship with his wife-who-wasn't (there were rumours of a love child). They challenged him on the lines of 'you, as a Christian'. He was absolutely honest. He was prepared to answer questions in a straight and humble way. He had the boys eating from the palm of his hand. His transparent honesty and goodwill really did have them exactly where he wanted them.

"Obviously he had a very deep faith. I'd almost call him a born-again Catholic. He'd been nurtured in his faith, but somehow we all gained the impression that at some stage in his life it had become renewed and he had found a *very* deep faith. Born-again is an extreme term, but one felt somehow or other that he had recovered his faith. A very wonderful man. The other thing that came through was his care of the less fortunate. He told a story or two of the people on his continent and their degradation and he was very moving about that.

> We all gained the impression that at some stage his faith had been renewed

"At the dinner we got on totally. I mean by that there was no barrier of any sort. We exchanged stories as much as anything. He acknowledged me for what I was and I did the same to him. He had this amazing ability to treat you as a friend from the word go. That was the naturalness, the sheer naturalness, of the man. It was wonderful, enchanting, and it enchanted the young people as well."

The school magazine, *The Lorettonian*, described the visit thus: "Mr Senna gave an instructive yet informed talk to the School on his life in F1 Motor Racing. He was a relaxed and genial guest, yet highly professional, dealing thoroughly with possibly the longest post-lecture question session for some time. Despite an intense schedule – he had to be in Portugal early the following day – Ayrton Senna happily gave his time and attention to all whom he met during his visit."

These Estoril tests, incidentally, were the very ones where Senna was (in context) scathing about the Honda V12 engine which he'd last tried in October. "It seemed to be going well then. I don't know what they have been doing since, but

Thumb nail sketch (Allsport).

there is not enough progress and not enough power." To say this publicly and about the notoriously sensitive Japanese – who were putting millions upon millions of dollars into development – was either a political move to make them work harder or maybe just the plain truth. Maybe both.

(The love-child 'situation' still lurks in the background as I write these words in early spring 1995. A 28-year-old former model, Marcella Praddo, claimed Senna was the father of her daughter Victoria. She hired a leading lawyer, Michel Assef, to take her case to law. There was talk of DNA tests – genetic characteristics which seem conclusive to a remarkable degree of accuracy – but whether such tests have been carried out nothing is known. Praddo doesn't say and Assef doesn't say. Nor do they say anything about anything else. A local journalist rings Praddo's number regularly and gets no reply, same with Praddo's mother. The nearest he has been is that a friend of Praddo, who attended Victoria's first birthday party, on 7 September 1994, said there could be no doubt she was Senna's daughter. What is the 'situation'? Praddo, approached by a British newspaper and offered $10,000 for an interview, declined. One theory is that she doesn't want a cut of Senna's millions, only to legitimise Victoria. Another theory is that she doesn't need money. A third theory is that it may never come to court because these things can take many years and, in comparison to Brazil, the Italian legal system is incisive, speedy and straightforward. A fourth theory is that it may come to court but only when the participants are much older. A fifth theory . . .)

By nature, Senna was protective of his religious beliefs because "often I was misquoted or misinterpreted." The result was an accumulation of general statements he'd made on the subject, or endless conjecture that he spent a lot of his time on aeroplanes and at race tracks reading the Bible.

For instance, in a 1989 interview with Anne Giuntini in the French sportspaper *L'Equipe* he was asked about the link between motor racing, God and himself. This is what he replied: "It is everything. I am permanently seeking perfection. I want to improve in every respect. I spend my time pushing back limits. I like to constantly go further, to solve problems. The big challenge for me is always to find better solutions than other people. I want to be capable of doing better than other people. At the same time I feel that I possess a kind of strength that brings me nearer to God. It is difficult to explain, but it is what I feel. And I am lucky to have found this route to such a state of harmony.

"I want to learn and to know everything that faith can bring me, and to make other people understand it in the same way. Many people don't succeed in finding contentment because, in the world in which we live, what's white is white and what's black is black. And one final point. I would like to provide concrete proof that we can really push back our limits, that this strength we can find in ourselves does enable us to improve constantly."

Thereby hangs another tale. It happened to Joe Saward, then of *Autosport*, and it happened in what might appear a curious way, although in purely journalistic terms it wasn't. Securing interviews with celebrities is by no means an exact science.

In the 8 October 1992 issue of *Autosport*, Saward wrote an open letter to Senna. During the season, Senna had tried to join Williams, who were rumoured to have lured Prost from retirement for 1993. Senna claimed Prost blocked him joining the team and claimed, too, that this had been done "in a cowardly way," meaning Prost is frightened of having me as a partner.

The Adelaide cartoon by Stonie which appeared long before my book of the same name (courtesy of John Stoneham of Top Draw).

Saward wrote: "Everything is relative in Formula 1, isn't it? Look at your talent, for example. All those blokes out there are bloody good, even the ones driving the cars which do not qualify for the races. Racing reporters (who needs them, eh?) may sit around and discuss the finer points of Formula 1 drivers and their talents, but the truth is that you are all super-talented. It is just the extra few thousandths of a second which is worth all that lovely money which you superstars collect, as opposed to the debts that some of the pay-drivers manage to bury themselves under.

"What am I trying to say? Well, let's face it, everyone is expendable. You know that Formula 1 needs you and, I suppose, this gives you bargaining power, but remember – always remember – that back in the bad old days stars died more often than they retired and there were always new stars. There are new stars standing behind you now. OK, perhaps they are pale shadows of what you are but they are stars nonetheless. I do hope you were just posturing when you said you'd quit if you didn't get a good car . . .

I hope you were just posturing when you said you'd quit if you didn't get a good car

"And another thing. I don't understand this 'Prost is a coward' business. Far be it for me to remind you, but a few years ago, when a Mr. Warwick wanted to join Team Lotus, you blocked his arrival. You may say that Lotus wasn't capable of running two cars at the time and you were doing Derek a favour – look, you could argue, what happened to the man who became your team-mate, Johnny Dumfries."

Saward concluded: "Remember when Fangio said you were a great champion but not a great sportsman. And you said you would try to achieve that. Well, I don't think this is the way to achieve that goal. See you in Australia." That, of course, was the Australian Grand Prix on 8 November, last of the season.

During race weekend at Adelaide, Lee Guag, long-time Goodyear tyre man, had a farewell party and Saward says "Ayrton and I were sitting opposite one another. I'd written the Open Letter which basically said 'stop messing about and get on with the driving' and this had been faxed to him about 15 times by Jo Ramirez because Jo Ramirez thought he should read it. At some point down the line Ayrton obviously had read it, as he did read things, and was upset. About half way through the dinner – and we were supposed to be bidding goodbye to Lee, who was sitting there with pneumonia – Ayrton suddenly said 'why do you write this rubbish?'"

Saward: "I wrote it because it's true."

Senna: "No, it's not."

Saward: "If it's not true, prove it to me."

Senna: "It's not true. Why should I trust the press?"

Saward: "Well, why don't you try? Have you tried it with me?"

Senna: "No, I haven't."

Saward: "OK, try it with me sometime."

Like a good and dogged journalist, Saward made a formal application for a personal interview with Senna (via Betise Assumpcao) "months and months and months" in advance of it actually taking place. Very often, it is what you had to do. A mass Press Conference was a different matter, but the rarity of a one-on-one was something else and, from Senna's point of view, a genuine concession to be carved out of the valuable moments over a race weekend. En masse, he was getting the thing over with for everybody all at once. If he tried to satisfy every individual

140

request, the whole weekend would be swallowed *at every Grand Prix*. He'd have lacked the time to go near the car, never mind drive it.

In fact, Saward only got the interview by default. "He wouldn't do the one-on-one but Betise put me together with, I think, some Belgian journalists who really didn't have that much grasp of English. This was at the Hungaroring in August 1993, eight months after Adelaide. It must have been following a qualifying session because Senna wore his racing gear. I remember that it had been an extremely hot day, it gets clammy-hot there and so the paddock cleared very quickly. Basically, the paddock was clear of all the wombats (hangers-on constantly coming up to Senna).

ABOVE LEFT Words, with Joe Saward.

ABOVE Juan-Manuel Fangio making a point, forcibly.

"We sat at a table outside the McLaren motorhome. There were two or three questions from the others, about his feelings on McLaren and so forth, then they just sat there. I said to him at the start 'I want it to be nothing to do with motorsport, I'm not interested in that on this particular occasion'. It began in a very *bristly* way, because we'd known each other for about 10 years without really talking. We talked about sex, religion, education, politics and he also talked about leaving McLaren. Did I raise the matter of religion or did it just gravitate to that? We discussed the non-motor racing related topics that human beings discuss and it came up because it was a very important part of his life, and one which I think was much underestimated. What Senna was doing was trusting a journalist, and he was trusting me because I'd said 'give me a chance before you judge me'. It was good of him, it really was." The discussion continued, as Saward remembers, "until we ran out of time because it got dark!"

Autosport carried the interview extensively and it included these Senna words: "I have

The true pal, Berger, here with designer Steve Nichols (John Townsend).

been questioned many times about religion and often I was misquoted or misinterpreted. Sometimes it was by accident, sometimes to do me damage, but I think it is worth talking about because in this godless world there are lots and lots of people looking for religion. They are desperate for it. I am only being truthful. I am saying what I believe and what I feel. You offer religion to those who want it. If you don't do that, they will not have the opportunity to look and see. Some people may not understand you and do not have a clear opinion, some will understand because they are open enough to understand what you are talking about. It is for them that it is worth it.

"You can have it if you want. It is a question of believing it and having faith, of wanting it and being open to the experience. I think there is an area where logic applies and another where it does not. No matter how far down the road you are in understanding and experiencing religion, there are certain things which we cannot logically explain. We tend always to understand what we can see: the colours, the touch and the smell. If it is outside that, is it crazy? I had the great opportunity to experience something beyond that. Once you have experienced it, you know it is there, and that is why you have to tell people.

"You have to need it and you have to want it and you have to be open to it. It is tough, but life isn't easy. Anyone can achieve easy things: the tough ones are things that some achieve and some do not. I am still at the beginning. I am like a baby in this respect. You have to work on it. It is a difficult thing and it is much more difficult alone." He added: "You can be logical or stupid but you are not in control of everything that is happening with your life."

Now, perhaps, you understand what the Bishop of Truro meant, and why he began his sermon at Loretto as he did.

Later in the interview Senna said "we go into millions of homes by way of television and people feel close to us, but at the same time they are far away. They have no idea what we are really like. They dream of watching a race live or getting to see one of us and perhaps if they had the opportunity they would see that we are just people, that there is nothing magic."

Yes, never claimed to be more or less.

"The wealthy can no longer continue to live on an island in a sea of poverty. We are all breathing the same air. People have to have a chance, a basic chance at least." He talked of marriage and children. "That will happen when I have the right girl and we feel it is the right moment for us."

Thereby hangs another tale, and one which I relate with a certain caution because it cropped up almost inadvertently in conversation with an FIA official. At the time, the official and his partner wanted a child and were considering adoption. The official was at a test session at Silverstone, was in the McLaren motorhome and mentioned it to Senna who, as he remembers, "immediately picked up his mobile phone, rang his sister in Brazil and started to organise it!" The official quietened him, saying they were only considering adoption.

The most obvious interpretation is that Senna would instinctively try and help someone over something so important. The official and I mull it over and we conclude that, all in the moment, Senna's logic unfolded in two directions simultaneously.

1) Here is someone I can help.

2) In doing so, I can give one Brazilian orphan not just a chance nor just a basic chance but a very good chance.

Therefore, where's my phone?

There can be no doubt that Ayrton Senna experienced terrible

Senna at Loretto with Daniel Davidson, a prefect, next to the Jim Clark plaque (Loretto School).

disquiet when he surveyed the poverty of his own country, a disquiet compounded because he witnessed it getting worse. There can be no doubt either that he experienced the anguish of helplessness because even his will-power, even his multi-millions, even the use of his all-pervading name could never alleviate the plight of so many impoverished souls existing one remove from animals.

He'd try with the *Senninha* comic to give kids something to strive for, maybe convince them that they could not only strive but succeed whatever odds were heaped against them in the wreckage and ruin of the *favelas*. A certain logic here, too. Virtually the only exit from these *favelas* was petty crime or becoming a footballer, the latter much easier at the outset than motor racing because you only really need boots (and could, literally at a pinch play barefoot, as Brazilian kids do on the beach). But even football is not an easy path once it starts to get serious.

Romario, the Brazilian striker – a member of the side which won the World Cup in the United States in mid-summer 1994 and promptly dedicated it to Senna's memory – says: "I come from a poor family. Sometimes I had to miss training so that my brother could go. We couldn't both afford to go. We had very little money. I'm sure this is still the case today. There are many young players who are not seen at the clubs because they can't afford the bus fare to get to the training."

Senna knew, as everybody knows, that if you can't raise a bus fare the prospect of buying a kart is beyond imagination, but he must also have known that his career represented something else beyond money. If you set out to achieve and you are determined enough, you can achieve it virtually whatever obstacles are put in your way. True, he'd had more than enough money to get the kart, enough to come to England for the single-seaters, but thereafter many obstacles stood in his way: homesickness, an active dislike of the soggy English climate, learning a foreign language, the choice of sustaining his marriage or his career. Further obstacles followed: the struggles with Piquet, Prost and Mansell for the World Championship and becoming the man every other driver wanted to beat. Money always helps in daily life, just as a British Aerospace HS125 helps, but no amount of money could bring Brazil closer to England or make England a sunny, jet-ski place or make Piquet, Prost and Mansell and the others easier to beat; but he did win and it came from himself.

A footnote. One time Senna was visiting Professor Watkins at the London hospital and, no doubt, savouring the prospect of a Chinese meal in anonymity. As he waited for Watkins to become free, an elderly patient in a wheelchair needed moving from one department to another. Guess who volunteered to push the wheelchair and did push it?

It was the same man who reached Tamburello on 1 May 1994 and had no more than 1.8 seconds of conscious thought or action left to him.

> It's as if the world changed shape when we weren't looking

Yes, a long year since yesterday afternoon. Monday, 2 May 1994, as Lyn Patey relates, "was a waste of time" at Silverstone. "We had the opening round of the International F3000 Championship and rounds 5 and 6 of the British Formula 3 Championship to get through. The drivers were going through the motions, everybody was holding themselves in check. The Brazilians were particularly affected, but all the drivers were deeply, deeply in shock. David Coulthard showed incredible restraint and dignity when he was approached by some creature who gave him a pally slap to the shoulder and declared, 'that's you in the second (Williams) seat, then!'

"There had been tears, lots of tears. In the paddock a friend, never a particular fan of Ayrton, put a consoling arm around my shoulders and said 'it's as if the world changed shape when we weren't looking'. One by one the winners disclaimed all interest in their victories in the circumstances. Work had to be got through and it was a huge relief to get away, to get home and to be private. Then came the first inklings of the enormity of our loss. Have we finally found a replacement for the Kennedy assassination in term's of global awareness of one man's passing? In years to come will people from all around the world, from all walks of life, be able to answer the question 'do you remember where you were and what you were doing when you heard that Senna had died?' I think so."

On the Wednesday before Monaco, 10 days on from Imola and as the gathering for the Grand Prix began, the Senna family issued a statement to answer the thousands upon thousands of messages of condolence they had received, some from as far as Afghanistan.

For many years people from all over the world have shared with us their great admiration for our dear Ayrton Senna; someone who worked to make dreams come true, someone who always tried to improve in every aspect of his life; someone to whom life was filled with happiness;

someone who deeply loved his country. With the green and yellow flag of Brazil in his hands after each victory, Ayrton demonstrated with pride how much he believed in his country, and in his fellow Brazilian citizens who always loved and supported him. We now find comfort in our deepest belief that Ayrton's same ideals will endure throughout the world; ideals of solidarity and faith. God bless our friends from all nations who have demonstrated so much love and sympathy for us at this moment of pain and sorrow.

As the gathering increased, the banners began to appear at Monaco, as they would at every circuit before the long year ended. On the cliffs above the Principality, the first of them said AYRTON SENNA FOREVER. Down by the harbour, the usual vending stalls sold their usual souvenirs but Senna dominated them. One stall, devoted to tee-shirts of him, with the profits going to a Brazilian children's charity, sold out fast.

Joseph White of the *Associated Press* conducted a survey of the stalls and quoted a saleslady, Rachel Duffy, as saying, "I disagree with it, I disagree with making money on tee-shirts which are more expensive than the others just because it's Senna." White noted that Duffy was selling tee-shirts "emblazoned with the former three-times World Champion for $14 apiece – because her boss said she had to." White moved on and noted that other vendors lacked Duffy's inhibitions. Senna was everywhere: on hats, in photos, on scarves, his portrait woven into Brazilian flags. One stall estimated he accounted for 70% of what they were selling. A vendor said, "it's money. It's sad, but people want to pay their money. It's business." White concluded that "Ratzenberger, who lived in Monte

BELOW An inspiration for youngsters.

BELOW RIGHT Withdrawing far into himself, 1989.

Carlo, seemed to be the forgotten driver." He asked more than 12 vendors if they had *anything* on Ratzenberger and they told him, "no, not at all."

Approaching Monaco, drivers kept their personal barriers up in their own ways but two of them – Berger and Schumacher – publicly confessed they felt a pressing need to demonstrate to themselves that they could still drive a Formula 1 car as they had done before Imola. Berger had not fundamentally tampered with the decision he made at Imola to continue, although he'd missed a Ferrari testing session before Monaco because he didn't feel he could get in a car again yet; and Schumacher reacted by asking himself a series of profound questions about what he'd do if the feeling was wrong.

If either judged that something subconscious was holding them back, that the precious thousandths of a second were no longer there, they'd have to reconsider. Those thousandths are hewn from *absolute* commitment of the kind Senna had always shown everywhere but especially at Monaco. And Monaco hammered and haunted, anyway, as if time hadn't begun its healing process but reversed it. In the Thursday morning free practice, the Austrian Karl Wendlinger crashed in his Sauber, sustained serious head injuries and would lie for days in a coma at a Nice hospital, his life in danger. The barriers went up again.

And somehow they forced themselves through qualifying, forced themselves to the absolute commitment, went in search of the thousandths. This can't be emphasised too strongly. Monaco – an awkward place which punishes mistakes because it is so narrow – measures 2.068 miles (3.328 kilometres). This is the span from the third to the sixth row of the grid:

Christian Fittipaldi	1m 21.053s
Gianni Morbidelli	1m 21.189s
Martin Brundle	1m 21.222s
Pierluigi Martini	1m 21.288s
Ukyo Katayama	1m 21.731s
Michele Alboreto	1m 21.793s

To make this comprehensible for an everyday motorist is difficult. Fittipaldi's time represented a very good performance (sixth fastest overall) while Alboreto's – slower by such a ridiculously fleeting margin over the 2.068 miles – represented comparative failure (eleventh fastest overall). Failure? At Monaco, overtaking is notoriously fraught and mostly impossible unless the driver in front permits it. Across the years, Monaco has been littered with the wreckage of those who tried without permission. Only Senna might have had a chance of winning from eleventh, however unlikely, because drivers would get out of his way: part respect for him, part intimidation by his reputation. They knew he might not wait for permission . . .

In the background, moves on safety intensified and would come to represent one of the legacies of Senna and, however unprovable, the legacy of Ratzenberger. Some things have to be faced. I do not believe the death of Ratzenberger alone would have lent such urgency to this, or made it such an imperative, but Senna and Tamburello had become a world-wide matter, and what had passed for 12 years as another sporting activity among many found itself under ferocious scrutiny and questioning.

After Imola, the Italian defence minister, Fabio Fabbri, was quoted as saying: "I hope the murder of Imola is punished. The Formula 1 world is worse than the gladiator's circus." Italian President Oscar Luigi Scalfaro sent a telegram to the President

The Brazilian World Cup team dedicate their victory to Senna at the Rose Bowl, Pasadena, summer 1994.

of Brazil stating his disapproval that the race had not been abandoned after Senna's crash. The Vatican newspaper, *L'Osservatore Romano*, wrote that "the show at Imola went on despite everything and death itself was made into a brutal spectacle." In a sense, these were instant reactions, however understandable. How could these people suddenly grasp that *it had always been like this, that the risks weren't new but eternal, that deep down every driver knew the score, that Grand Prix racing could be wonderfully rewarding but horrifically hard?*

At Monaco, amidst the grim, sombre, withdrawn faces, Niki Lauda announced the re-formation of the Grand Prix Drivers' Association to occupy itself with safety. Max Mosley, President of the FIA, said firmly that whatever was necessary would be done.

Before the start of the race, the drivers stood across the grid and observed a minute's silence. Two drivers held a large, square Brazilian motif: a green background, Senna's face against a segment of yellow and the simple message *adeus Ayrton*. When the cars formed up for the green light, the front row of the grid was left empty as a mark of respect. Williams ran only one car, for Damon Hill. Brazilian flags hung limp from balconies.

As these cars formed up for the green light, an uncounted number of regular telespectators around the world could not bring themselves to watch. Something had gone, and wasn't coming back: Senna's five pole positions here, some extraordinary, some challenging credulity; Senna's six victories here, some lusty and brave, some soothed by finesse. Many people, to judge from the letters I've received, would take months to watch again. Some never would.

Schumacher won Monaco, came second in Spain, won Canada on 12 June, the world moving on. The World Cup Finals began in the United States five days later. Romario's goal-scoring partner Bebeto was asked who he'd dedicate ultimate victory to if Brazil achieved that. He replied, "to my wife, my children, my family and above all to the Brazilian people. These suffering people have to have some happiness in their lives. Here in the United States, in the concentrated situation we find ourselves in, we never forget Brazil and I never forget Rio, which I love. More often than not, the players talk about it. Our people have had only blows – inflation, violence and corruption. Ah, I almost forgot. I will also dedicate the title to Ayrton Senna, a great idol who the people will never forget."

And it happened thus, not just from Bebeto but other players as well. The World Cup Final, between Brazil and Italy at the Rose Bowl, Pasadena, California, lurched to a penalty shoot-out and Roberto Baggio of Italy crucially missed his. In the commentary area, Pele – an icon like Senna – danced up and down in delight and shook his fist in triumph. The Brazilian players spilt onto the pitch and abandoned themselves to emotion. Romario, close to tears, was wrapped in a Brazilian flag. Then four, five, six players held a banner up to the crowd. It was white with a message in black full across. *Senna: we accelerate together. The fourth title is yours.* Brazil won the World Cup in 1958, 1962 and 1970 so this was the fourth. Senna won the World Championship in 1988, 1990 and 1991 so 1994 might have been his fourth.

The long year limped on and at race after race the Senna flags and banners fluttered, plaques were set up, statues unveiled, homage paid because each race was the first in each place without him, the grief and void coming afresh to each group of supporters: Magny-Cours, Silverstone, Hockenheim, the Hungaroring, Spa; and at Spa, wonderfully, Barrichello took pole position in the Jordan. He had not been on pole before and neither had Jordan. In a wet-but-drying session he timed his most important run perfectly

BELOW LEFT Hill is given a World Cup-winning shirt because the team wanted him to have it as Senna's last partner.

BELOW Thanking those who kept the faith. Viviane Lalli at the Japanese Grand Prix.

and dedicated the pole to Senna.

Schumacher took the title in Adelaide and, in turn, dedicated it to Senna. Schumacher and Hill had crashed, of course, but by tradition Schumacher, as the new Champion, took his place with the first three in the Australian Grand Prix, Mansell, Berger and Brundle. Martin Whitaker, handling the televised interviews, said to Schumacher: "World champion – the first German in the Championship's 45 year history, but there are a lot of people, including yourself, who would not have wished to see the championship decided in this way."

Schumacher: "Certainly. I mean, it was a very great battle between me and Damon at that stage of the race. I would say it was thrilling for you on the outside." Schumacher then apologised to Hill about earlier comments he'd made, and finished: "But I have something special to say about this whole season. It started quite well in Brazil, even Aida it was a good race, and then we came up to Imola (shakes head). What happened at Imola is just a . . . (purses lips, shakes head again) . . . all of us know what kind of feelings we had to make about this, particularly for Ayrton but also for Roland and as well for Karl – what happened in Monte Carlo. For me it was always clear that I was not going to win the Championship and it was Ayrton who was going to win the Championship, but he hasn't been there for the last races. I'd like to take this Championship and give it to him because he is the driver who should have earned it. He had the best car, he was the best driver . . ."

That was mid-November. A month later the second Elf Master Karting took place at Bercy. Sometimes, time passed quickly in the long year. Could it have been a whole 12 months since Senna was here with Adriane? Yes, but it felt like yesterday evening.

Philippe Streiff says "every driver wore the *Senninha* logo as a mark of respect." Prost had the distinctive *S* on his left arm and, throughout the event when he wasn't driving, sported a *Senninha* cap. Good men and true attended Bercy and drove there: Prost, Schumacher, David Coulthard, Herbert, Alessandro Zanardi, Olivier Panis and several young hopefuls. The indoor course, so tight that the racing was nip and tuck and nudge, proved ideal for real racing, just as Ayrton Senna would have wished. Schumacher, who reportedly brought a team of mechanics from Germany, won, Prost third.

"Before the presentations," Streiff says, "all the lights were switched off and we had three minutes of absolute silence – 15,000 people and no sound. Then Alain Prost paid a very touching homage about how Ayrton was here only last year and how much he was missed."

Prost said: "Last year, Ayrton was in our midst, competing here. He was here because he had a passion for the sport, a very deep passion, which drove him to look for perfection. We all have a similar feeling, which helps us to go on when terrible things happen."

Streiff ruminates on the three minutes of silence. "The event was televised by *Eurosport* and obviously because we were to switch all the lights off, you can't very well have three minutes of the silence and what would have been a blank screen. So we'd compiled our tribute in pictures and that was transmitted. It was condensed from 32 minutes of film from the year before and you can see how happy he was, how full of happiness. That's strange, because in all the pictures of him I saw in 1994 – at the Brazilian Grand Prix, at Aida, before the race at Imola – he looked . . . sad.

RIGHT Marcella Praddo, who claims Senna fathered her daughter Victoria.

INSET Praddo and Victoria (John Townsend).

At Imola, he looked very sad.

"After Bercy in December 1994 his sister Viviane gave me a card, a card of good wishes. It had a picture of *Senninha* with the S large and a light coming from above it. On the card was written: 'Life is a gift from God every morning, and it is necessary for each and every person to rediscover the magic and mystery of life itself.'"

Owen O'Mahony refracts this, distils it into eight words, this same Owen O'Mahony who'd flown him so far and come to know him so well.

"Ayrton Senna was big enough to be little."

Late January-early February 1995 and the long year will complete itself in just a few weeks. The Liveranis are reluctant to speak about Senna because, I sense, they feel close to him and maybe are expecting to see him in that small, private dining room again. They are extremely unanxious to promote the Romagnola restaurant through his association with it. Paolo, one of the two brothers running it, does speak and in a few moments he's very close to breaking down. His eyes look away, then at the floor as he composes himself. When he's done that he recounts an anecdote which still amuses him.

Once, just once, Senna arrived – it was a test session at Imola – and they couldn't give him the private room because it was already full. For some reason Senna hadn't forewarned them he'd be coming. They asked if he'd mind going into the main dining room and he said he wouldn't mind. Of course the other diners there wanted his autograph and he handled that with his usual grace. However, one of the autograph hunters tried to lure him into signing a blank cheque.

"Sorry, no chance!"

I imagine the place shook with laughter.

The walls of the Romagnola are full of pictures of disabled pushchair races around Castel San Pietro, but no pictures of Senna, no proclamations that the great Ayrton Senna was a patron, nothing except, discreetly on one wall, his autograph on a sheet of the block notepad. "It's a photocopy," Paolo says. "I've got the original locked safely away."

Apart from the privacy of the small room, apart from the food, apart from the family embrace which the Liveranis exuded, I wonder if Senna kept going there *because* it did not have pictures and proclamations of himself; didn't have posters of that yellow helmet and the red and white Marlboro McLaren or the blue and white Rothmans Williams leaping off the walls at him – as they did in so many other places on earth, cafes, bars, factories, bedrooms, living rooms, airports, magazine stands, hoardings.

We'll never know now.

The Hotel Castello has experienced a sharp dilemma over Room 200. A lot of people ring up and say they want to stay in it. Others – when told its significance – say they don't want to stay in it. If someone arrives and wants a suite and obviously doesn't know, the reception is drawn between telling them and not telling them. I sense they haven't quite resolved this dilemma yet.

The circuit of Imola is deserted this winter's day. A few of the permanent staff are working in offices in the long building above the pits, which is next to the control tower. There is a map of the revised circuit, the alterations intended to be in

RIGHT *A season of memorials.*

"RACING, COMPETING, IS IN MY BLOOD, IT'S PART OF ME, IT'S PART OF MY LIFE."
AYRTON SENNA

maig de 1994

AYRTON SENNA

"CÓRRER, COMPETIR, HO PORTO A LA SANG, ÉS UNA PART DE MI, DE LA MEVA VIDA".

"CORRER, COMPETIR, TENHO-O NO SANGRE, FAZ PARTE DE MIM MESMO, FAZ PARTE DA MIHA VIDA".

"CORRER, COMPETIR, LO LLEVO EN LA SANGRE, ES PARTE DE MI, ES PARTE DE MI VIDA".

AYRTON SENNA

*A season of memories.
This is Hill at Spa
(Empics).*

place when the year completes itself. The San Marino Grand Prix would fall, in 1995, on 30 April, a day short of the calendar completion.

The map shows alterations to about half the circuit but helplessly your eye is drawn to Tamburello. It will become an S-bend – left-right-left – and the new section of track will coil away from the wall; there'll be a proper gravel trap, deep enough to stop a car in good time; and, anyway, the cars will be passing through at the reduced speed an S-bend demands. The old Tamburello will be a memory, seared and searing, but a memory.

This deserted winter's day, you can walk from the grid to Tamburello as it still is. It's not a long walk. You pass under the gantry bestriding the track which houses the red stop lights and the green go lights, the last ones he saw. You follow the little left-hand corner where, at the start of the race yesterday afternoon, he had already taken the lead for the last time. You're out into the country, which is actually a public park, the track slicing through. On the other side of the wire fencing, a group of old men chuckle and argue at an intersection. Ordinary cars pass quietly by because a normal road runs there, just the other side. Joggers pass, too. A man in a woollen hat whistles for his dog and it scampers through undergrowth towards him.

Just for a moment, the contrast is difficult to take. Five or six yards away, the most normal, mundane, everyday form of life is going on. *Here* the ribbon of track so accustomed to unimaginable ferocity is entirely empty. Yes, *here* are the verdant trees he saw, the strips of grass, the white boundary line whose coats of paint have crusted and cracked a bit. And up *there* ahead, *there* a couple of hundred yards away is the red and white kerbing to the left, the advertising hoardings to the right and the tightness, the narrowness, the on-and-on out-of-sight final twist of Tamburello.

I suppose, during those 200 yards, I was walking towards him and walking back to myself and, just for a moment, that contrast was difficult to take, too. I started writing about Formula 1 in 1982, started writing about him in 1983 as a man I'd soon be writing about in Formula 1. As I'm nearing Tamburello I have in my pocket a little green book for telephone numbers and his is in there, circa 1983, a Tilehurst, Berkshire, number. I hadn't taken the book deliberately, because I take it everywhere, but somehow the phone number returned me virtually to when I'd begun: I'd spent every year except 1982 writing about him.

As I'm nearing Tamburello, a little flurry of memories came back. Silly memories, mostly. Human memories. Stowe corner, Silverstone, one time and we're discussing his braking point in the Marlboro McLaren and where mine would be in my Ford Sierra. I indicate mine. "That's a long way back," he says. "Funny," I say, "I thought it was too close." Another time I've scribbled some practice lap times in a notebook and he beckons me over, wants to see what the others are doing. My scribble is spaghetti carbonara with a felt-tipped pen but he locks onto the numerals and dissects them as if he's moved into another world: of analysis, received information, conclusions. He nods and hands the notebook back. He *knows* now and he's stored it.

Another time I'm putting together a Grand Prix supplement for the *Daily Express* prior to the British Grand Prix and wouldn't it be interesting to get him *batting at cricket?* I'm curious to see how fast he masters the mechanisms of something completely unfamiliar, how his co-ordination copes with pads, gloves, a bat and a moving ball. I explain this and he says "sure, ring me." The supplement didn't have enough space for the article and so the cricket never happened.

Viviane Lalli in London, winter, 1994 (Times Newspapers Limited).

It's normal, I believe, with any bereavement that you remember what had been and equally mourn what hadn't been and now never would be.

Another time further on down the road, Donington 1993, the Thursday before the European Grand Prix when, on the Sunday in the wet, he will make his own contribution to Einstein's Theory of Relativity. He espies me lurking and, as usual, moves to shake hands because he was, all else aside, an instinctively polite man. I shoo him off because I'm streaming and steaming with influenza of the virulent weak-at-the-knees kind and the last thing I want is for him to catch it. What if we had shaken hands and he had caught it? What if *even he* was too weakened-at-the-knees to construct the great, majestic, mental arithmetic race which he did, a race so enormous in execution and accomplishment that it takes its place among the greatest ever driven by anyone?

Ah, well.

Like I say, mostly silly memories.

It's a crisp, cloudless winter's day, a little wind stirring the parched leaves which have gathered, nestling, against the wall at Tamburello. In the wall there is a gouge mark, the sort you'd expect shrapnel to make: not symmetrical but a frantic, shapeless burst into the eight inches of concrete. It is not very large. On the wall, like a form of graffiti touched with grace, are messages of salute and condolence and devotion in several languages. A man and a woman from Holland have inscribed in English *Senna for always in our minds 26-1-95*. Above the wall, slotted into the wire mesh, are bouquets. The most touching is a single tulip whose stem has been crudely hand-wrapped in a twist of ordinary tinfoil. It's easy to buy a bouquet but to pick a tulip and arrange it yourself seems quite different: humble and thoughtful and entirely personal, *my gesture to you*. There's no card attached to it, no message, just the tulip bending to the wind.

> There's no card, no message, just a tulip bending to the wind

A bouquet has fallen into the leaves and they partially camouflage it, rustling and whispering around it; some leaves scrape over the concrete run-off area away from the wall, away from the wall. The wind rises to a gusting flurry so that, in unison, all the bouquets except the one which has fallen are beating hard against the wire-mesh above the wall.

It was a long walk back.

When I get home, I'm speaking on the telephone to Barrichello and, however painful Imola might be to discuss, he readily agrees to help get some of the detail correct. During this conversation, my daughter is trying to get through to say she's had a car crash. She keeps on trying and the moment I put the phone down on Barrichello it rings and there she is. She's OK but the car isn't. On a left-right section of a country road the car may have hit black ice. She wrestled it and it clipped kerbing, was airborne, ran across a corner of a field, burst a substantial wooden fence and reared up a bank towards a concrete wall. The ground was heavy, muddy, cloying. The car stopped just short of the wall.

A few days further on, I'm chatting to O'Mahony and he's remembered another anecdote. It centres on Imola and the traditional testing there well before the San Marino Grand Prix. Senna had a hire car, O'Mahony had a hire car and, the testing over, Senna wanted his baggage transferred from his to O'Mahony's for transport to the aeroplane. Senna would be coming along to the plane later, after a debrief. The baggage comprised a suitcase, a holdall and Senna's briefcase. *Don't take your eyes off the briefcase*, Senna instructed. O'Mahony began the transfer, lugging the suitcase, then the holdall, but when he returned to the boot of Senna's car a third time it was empty. Someone had stolen the briefcase. Seeing his career as Senna's pilot passing before his very eyes, as drowning men see their whole lives, he looked up and a *lot* of people were looking at him and his visible anxiety. Any of them might have done it, or an accomplice, or someone who'd run off – run off with Senna's money and passport and credit cards and helicopter pilot's licence and all else which the briefcase contained. Slowly, slowly those who looked at O'Mahony began to smile and that turned to laughter. Behind the bonnet of Senna's hire car a familiar figure bobbed up to have a swift savour of O'Mahony's anxiety, ducked down, bobbed up again. It was, of course, Senna and he had, of course, the briefcase he'd lifted unseen as O'Mahony did the lugging and he was, of course, grinning hugely. *I won't forget this*, O'Mahony said, *and I've a long memory*.

Ayrton Senna da Silva had a grin you'll never forget, anyway, and it always conveyed the same thing. Sunshine.

In February, the investigation into the crash still awaited, Frank Williams speaks of Senna, seeks out the Senna context. He's not sure about ultimate speed because "I've always thought Jochen Rindt (the Austrian World Champion, posthumously, 1970) was the quickest human being God ever created." Rindt drove for Lotus and, confining himself to his own drivers, Williams estimates "Ayrton was certainly the most competitive. In my opinion, Alain Prost was just as skilful – very, very skilful, immensely precise – but the difference was the commitment."

Question: Did you feel Senna had a strong shell with a brittle centre?

"Effectively, he only drove for Williams for two races and did some testing so I can't tell you very well. He was definitely the best driver who's ever driven for Williams. His mental application was remarkable, his ability to understand and improve the car was better than anybody else we've ever had, and in saying that I'm not denigrating the other drivers who came before him."

How did you cope as a person with Imola?

"You have to get on with your life."

I'm not sure I could cope.

"You would, if it happened to you. You've just got to get up in the morning and get on with it. Being busy is always the best antidote to events like that, the best antidote to mental distress."

Some time after yesterday afternoon, when the long year began, the children of Imola wrote poems and they were gathered into a book. It bears a simple title.

In paradise there are no walls.

Index